HO
ST
TOGETHER
FOREVER

HOW TO
STAY
TOGETHER
FOREVER

Julia Cole

Vermilion
LONDON

7 9 10 8 6

First published in the United Kingdom in 2003 by
Vermilion, an imprint of Ebury Press
Random House UK Ltd.

Ebury Publishing is a Random House Group company.

Random House UK Limited Reg. No. 954009

Addresses for companies within The Random House Group can be found at
www.randomhouse.co.uk

A CIP catalogue record is available for this book from the British Library

The Random House Group Limited supports The Forest Stewardship
Council (FSC), the leading international forest certification organisation.
All our titles that are printed on Greenpeace approved FSC certified paper
carry the FSC logo. Our paper procurement policy can be found at:
www.rbooks.co.uk/environment

Printed in the UK by CPI Cox & Wyman, Reading, RG1 8EX

ISBN 9780091887599

Copies are available at special rates for bulk orders. Contact the sales
development team on 020 7840 8487 or visit:
www.booksforpromotion.co.uk for more information.

To buy books by your favourite authors and register for offers, visit:
www.rbooks.co.uk

For Peter,
after twenty-five years of staying together

ACKNOWLEDGEMENTS

I wish to express my thanks to everyone who helped to make
this book possible:

To Lesley McOwan of Vermilion,
who encouraged and supported me
during the writing of the book.

To my agent Joanna Frank, whose wise advice
supports me in all my literary endeavours.

To my husband Peter, whose loving support
inspired and aided the production of the book
and to my daughter Hannah, who made me cups of tea
throughout the process.

CONTENTS

1
SHARE FEELINGS, HOPES, IDEAS AND DREAMS WITH YOUR PARTNER

In a loving relationship, talking and listening to your partner is the most important skill you require. If you can communicate with ease, everything else in your relationship will work. Good talking and listening skills are the basis of every committed partnership. Think of it like this. When you first enter the land of love it may not matter that you do not speak the language. You can probably get by on signs and gestures. But if you want to stay longer than a few days, you have to learn to speak the language. And each new relationship means learning a new language. As with foreign travel, learning French is good if you want to stay in France, but not if you move to China. You and your partner need to develop and learn a personal language – and I do not mean the pet names you give each other!

All successful relationships share one key attribute – the ability to share ideas and feelings even when things are tough. This is not to suggest that successful couples never argue. They do. But the arguments of secure couples lead to the successful resolution of problems rather than a continuing round of disagreement and recrimination. Talking and listening is something you will need to do throughout the lifetime of your relationship. If you stay together for some time, you will both change and so will your relationship. As with any skill, the more you talk about what you are interested in, and concerned about, the closer you will feel. Some couples become so adept at watching and understanding each other they can read what their partner is thinking by just looking at them. But this Nirvana of couple relating takes years of practice, and constant checking out that what you assume he/she is thinking is correct, before it feels natural.

So what are the benefits of creating a communicating relationship? Here are a few good reasons to keep talking.

Why communicating is good for you

Talking and listening to each other creates:

- A warm and intimate relationship. You will understand one another's desires and vulnerabilities and support each other through difficult times.
- A sense of belonging. You will feel that your partner knows you really well. This means that you will seek each other out to consult or celebrate with, giving a sense of security.
- The feeling that you are 'team players'. If you check out your decisions with each other and talk about everything, from how much money you should spend to who should wash the clothes, you will feel that your relationship is heading in the same direction rather than along two separate paths.
- A way of dealing with disagreements without too much friction. If you are used to talking about anything and everything, when you do disagree you will know how to discuss matters without inflaming a tense situation further.
- A safe harbour when you need it. If you experience job problems, a bereavement, or face an illness, knowing you have a listening and caring partner beside you can get you through the most taxing experience.

- A satisfying sex life. If you can talk about sexual matters without embarrassment, your sex life will be fun and meet your changing desires as your relationship develops.
- A good example for your children. This may not be the first thing you think of when you start learning to talk and listen to one another, but children learn what they live with. If you can talk to each other without constant crossed wires, they will use the same techniques with you and their friends, brothers and sisters. This makes family life much easier.

The rule is simple. Good communication makes a successful relationship. Poor communication breaks it. It has benefits in almost every area of life, giving you both the chance to feel less stressed and safe with one another. Given that the outcome of talking and listening effectively is so good, why is it that lots of people find it so hard to do?

Here's why lots of couples find talking to one another so difficult.

The Five Myths of Communication – why couples fail in communicating

Myth **1**

It is unromantic to have to spell out your hopes and expectations. True love means you understand each other without speaking.

Myth Busting

Hoping your partner notices how angry, miserable, happy or excited you are is a bit like playing the children's card game 'Pairs'. They may notice you seem a bit moody or talkative, but not put this together with the reason. Or if they grasp the reason, they may not connect that to the way you are behaving. Often, couples avoid tackling a partner who seems out of sorts because they fear being blamed for the problem. If you want support, advice or a shoulder to cry on, you must clearly say what is troubling you, what you need and why.

Myth 2

I know all about my partner and what they are going to say on a given subject. I've heard their every opinion on politics, religion, sex and the price of bread. There is no point in encouraging them to talk or listen to me because I could guess what they would say or do.

Myth Busting

You may think you know what they would say, but do you really know them as well as you think? When did you last try asking them for their ideas? Chances are you knew what they thought ten days, weeks or years ago, but do you really know what they are thinking today? Making assumptions about what your partner will do or say stops your relationship from growing. Plus, if you assume he/she has not changed or matured, they may eventually feel you do not know them at all. Checking out what your partner thinks, or asking them for help when you need it, allows you to build bridges of communication you can utilise even when you disagree.

Myth 3

I have tried sharing my joys and worries with my partner, but they seem to take very little notice. If I ask for them to change their behaviour towards me, they sometimes make

an effort for a short while but then things go back to the way they were. It's pointless even making the attempt.

Myth Busting

You might do a lot of asking, but do you do much giving? This view of communication is 'you' centred. What you get from it becomes the most important outcome. But what about your partner? They may feel that their needs are overlooked because what you want is always paramount. This is not communication. Good communication can only take place when you listen carefully to your partner's point of view as well as explaining what is going on in your head. They may have good reasons for not wanting to do what you are asking for, but you could have missed them because you have only focused on your personal desired outcome.

Myth 4

Sharing too many feelings destroys all sense of mystery between couples. It is important to maintain some distance between each other because otherwise the relationship becomes boring.

Myth Busting

If you want to be in a relationship, rather than a Ruth Rendell thriller, mystery will not do you any favours. OK, you may not want to shave your legs or use the loo while your partner is in the bathroom (although some do) but regular talking about your relationship is crucial if you want it to survive. Keeping secrets, or avoiding intimacy with your partner, is more likely to be connected to a fear of letting someone into your life than a bid to stay in love. Over time all relationships evolve and change. It is this that supplies the interest and excitement in a partnership rather than the maintenance of false barriers and keeping each other at arm's length to preserve passion.

Myth 5

Talking all the time turns you into brother and sister rather than lovers. Action is just as important as talking.

Myth Busting

There is some truth in this myth. But only some! Couples who spend their whole time talking and sharing, but taking no action, can find themselves in a vicious circle. They may talk for hours but still be no nearer to resolving a problem or taking a decision. So talking can seem like a trap rather than a release. But without discussion and debate it can be impossible to make a shared decision. Almost all couples eventually encounter the 'why did you do it?' row. They may have been trying to talk about buying a new sofa or car, only to discover a day or two later that their partner has rushed ahead and taken the decision. Talking through options before choices and events can help you to feel like a team, pulling together.

? How do I usually communicate with my partner?

Here is a quiz to help you understand the way in which you usually communicate with your partner. Once you have grasped your favoured method of communication, read the suggestions that could help you improve your behaviour so the two of you can talk more easily. Mark each question **a**, **b**, **c** or **d** according to which seems closest to your usual response.

 Your partner has a problem at work with a colleague. He/She is talking to you about their difficulty. Do you:

a) Offer lots of practical solutions.

b) Mentally rehearse what you would do in the situation because it could help.

c) Try to grasp what is going on by asking questions about the situation.

d) Listen and ask him/her to tell you what the key issues are.

2 You are trying to choose where to go on holiday. As you pore over the brochures you:

a) Ask your partner to tell you exactly what they think of each resort.

b) Sort the brochures into piles because you can guess what sort of holiday he/she wants.

c) Draw up a list of all the resorts with similarities to previous holidays you or friends have enjoyed.

d) Decide together what you are looking for before opening any brochure.

3 When you disagree you usually tend to:

a) Demand answers about problems from your partner. But you may become annoyed if they cannot supply you with the answers that you want.

b) Tell your partner what they ought to do, but then end up with a long cold silence if you disagree.

c) Decide you know what they are thinking and get upset if they behave in a way that is 'out of character'.

d) Try to calm things down but you may get frustrated if the situation boils over without any resolution.

4 You usually do your talking:

a) In snatched moments during the day. You look for quick answers rather than explore lots of options.

b) When you have all the facts or ideas in your head to present to your partner.

c) Over meal times or during social events when others may contribute to your discussions.

d) During quiet times at home.

5 The family you were brought up in was:

a) Busy and practical.

b) Serious and/or competitive.

c) Light hearted and fun loving.

d) Quiet and thoughtful.

6 In the past you have found talking:

a) OK, but limited. Sometimes it feels as if talking just confuses the issue.

b) Can be useful, but you often find it difficult to convince your partner of the right thing to do.

c) Helpful if you are with others who can offer their advice. Talking as a couple is sometimes frustrating.

d) Usually helpful in thinking through what has to be done or considered.

7 If your partner tells you good news you usually:

a) Want him/her to quickly tell you all the details of the news.

b) Need to understand how the news will affect you.

c) Immediately want to tell your relatives and friends.

d) Respond with congratulations and a display of affection.

8 You talk about sex:

a) Fairly infrequently. You would rather do it than talk about it!

b) When you are aware of a problem that is spoiling sex for you.

c) Hardly at all. You find it embarrassing to talk about sex.

d) Quite often. You can sort problems and say what you enjoy easily.

9 If you had to make a change in your talking and listening it would be:

a) For us to reach decisions more quickly.

b) To be listened to more.

c) To find it easier to talk when we are alone.

d) To find more time to talk.

10 I find talking to my partner:

a) Helpful, but I wish we could see more practical outcomes to our discussions.

b) Useful, but I would like more sense that my opinion matters to him/her.

c) OK, but I often feel we take in the opinions of others too readily.

d) An important part of our relationship. Without it, we would soon run into trouble.

Mostly **A**s

You are a practical person who tends to see talking with your partner as a means to an end rather than an open-ended exploration of feeling and thought. You look for decisions and outcomes that are easy to grasp and make sense of, rather than open-ended situations that leave room for complications and mistakes. This approach sometimes works to your advantage because you are often able to see what needs doing, but it can work against you. This is because leaping quickly to action can mean taking the wrong action. Listening and learning could really help you to improve your relationship. Your partner may also occasionally feel that you want to call all the shots. Sometimes they may be content to let this happen. In fact, they may have chosen you because you are a 'go-getting' sort of person. But they may also feel that you sometimes block their contribution to the relationship.

If this is you, improve your communication by:

- Deciding to slow your responses down. Ask fewer questions about practicalities and more about his/her feelings. For example, if your partner wants help in deciding which job he/she should go for, ask them what they feel about the post rather than offering lots of ideas about why he/she should, or shouldn't, take it.

- If your partner is having trouble explaining, avoid jumping in to end their sentences for them. Count to ten (or longer) so they have lots of space to find the right words for themselves.

- If you need to ask questions, use open-ended questions rather than closed questions. Instead of saying 'You like steak for dinner don't you?' (which can only be answered with a 'yes' or 'no') try starting your questions with 'How', 'Why', 'When' and 'What' to get more information. For example, 'What do you want for dinner?' allows your partner to explain what they really want.

- Listen carefully to your partner's answers. You may be in danger of deciding what he/she wants well before they have even started telling you their thoughts.

Mostly **B**s

You tend to think you know your partner really well – so well, in fact, that you think you know exactly what they want and what is best for them. You tend to see things from a very personal point of view. You probably think less about what your partner feels about a particular issue than what you think about it. This can look as if you are a very sure and focused person with set goals that you aim for. But it can also mean that you tend to believe that what you want should also be what your partner wants. You may find it hard to listen to your partner and take in what they say because of your set ideas about what should happen and when. This may be because you are, deep down, quite insecure and in need of being in control. You may even be afraid of allowing your partner to have a role in the relationship in case they decide to leave you.

If this is you, improve your communication by:

- Allowing your partner some space in daily decision making. Try starting with small items, for instance, choosing food at the supermarket or where to go for a meal, working up to larger choices such as where to go on holiday or which car to buy.

- Getting into the habit of asking your partner for their opinion. Switch off the tape that plays in your head telling you that you know better. Wait for their answer and think about what they have said. You may be tempted to dismiss their suggestions purely out of habit, so break the habit!

- Tackle the root cause of your control habit by asking yourself what you are scared of that could happen in the relationship if you relinquish some of the control. You may be worried that your partner will 'see through you', or that they will leave you if you do not keep tight hold of their rein. It could help to talk to a counsellor about your feelings.

- Allow yourself to sometimes do something a bit out of control. Experiment by eating unusual foods, listening to music you would normally avoid or watch a video you might not usually choose. Loosen up your usual constraints and you could find you feel less restricted when talking and listening to your partner.

Mostly **C**s

You like to think you know your partner well but sometimes feel surprised by his or her response. You also tend to canvass other people's opinions on issues and try to put these into the mix when talking and listening to your partner. This can be confusing for both of you as it can seem as if you have myriad voices in your head when trying to get to grips with a problem or decision. You may find yourself thinking what your best friend said, or how your parents reacted when you asked them for their opinion, instead of listening attentively to what your partner is saying. Sometimes it is useful to have other opinions to draw on, but if you constantly feel you need lots of other people involved in your communicating, you may be suffering from a lack of self-confidence. Or you may fear that your partner will find your opinion lacking in some way.

If this is you, improve your communication by:

- Improving your confidence in your ability to talk to your partner. Try taking a common situation you know you find hard to discuss. For example, imagine you want to see a band that is coming to play at your local theatre. Instead of asking your friends and relatives what they think of them, and whether this would be a good concert to go to, make a list of all the reasons *you* like them. Put down anything you feel is relevant. Now you have your list, talk to your partner about why you want to see the band. For example, you might say you liked them when you were younger, you have their CDs or you saw them on TV and thought they would sound good live. Ask your partner for his/her opinion, listening carefully to their response.

- Thinking about why you feel the need to involve other people in your communicating. You may be doing this because you feel close to your family and/or friends and rate their opinions as highly as your partner's. Or you may feel the need to have some kind of justification for what you want to say. But this could be getting in the way of your relationship, preventing you from forming an intimate partnership. It is possible that you are in the early stages of your relationship and learning to trust each other. As your trust grows, you should find you refer to others much less.

- Reflecting on talking and listening that has gone well in the past. Looking back, it was probably occasions when you were absorbed in one another rather than trying to talk in a crowd or with relatives. Build more time alone together. Have at least two evenings and one whole day together a week so you can build a sense of a couple relationship outside of other friendships.

Mostly **D**s

You are well practised at talking and listening to your partner and feel they listen responsively to you. It is likely you have been together for some while and feel comfortable saying almost anything to each other. You may wish you had more time to spend talking to one another, especially if you are both working full time. It is possible that you can be too reasonable, especially if you are trying to find a solution to a decision. A little more spontaneity in your relationship could help you to move forward if you are trying to be fair and polite towards each other. For instance, you may sometimes wish your partner would act rather than debate with you.

If this is you, improve your communication even more by:

- Lightening the mood a little when you talk. You may find that gentle humour could help your talking to feel less serious. But make sure you laugh *together*, not *at* each other.

- Building in times when you act more spontaneously. If you wake up on a sunny Saturday, seize the moment to go for a picnic or day out. You could also benefit from relaxing together more. Try long lie-ins or cosy evenings when you just enjoy a meal and each other's company.

- Listening to your heart. You may find you are the kind of person that spends a lot of time thinking about your partner and what they want from the relationship. It could improve your communication if you are occasionally a bit more up front about what you want and need.

Simple ways to quickly improve your talking and listening skills

Most people want to talk and listen well with their partners. But lots of people make simple mistakes about how to do this. Here are some ideas that will make an immediate and positive impact on your ability to talk and listen to your partner.

Put time aside

This probably sounds obvious. Without time to talk nothing can happen, but it's amazing how many couples spend years together avoiding talking time. They may put time aside to go to the pub, gym or to visit friends, but decide that talking to a partner should not need a particular time. This is true if your communication is top class – it should flow naturally at any time, but for most of us this is rarely true. What usually happens is that we try to grab a few moments between TV programmes (the 'ad break conversation') or just as one partner is dashing out the door to work. So if this sounds familiar, try this. Turn off the TV or CD for an hour a couple of evenings a week and just chat about what you have been doing and how you are feeling. Don't push for heavy-duty topics – just let the conversation find its own level. Once you are used to doing this, you will probably find that even subjects you dread talking about are easier to discuss. This is a habit that is good for you, but it requires practice. Keep up your conversation dates for a few weeks and your communication will improve dramatically.

You should also pick the right time. Never try to talk about anything in the half an hour 'bear with a sore head' phase as you both meet after work. Instead, change your clothes, have half an hour to yourselves, or quietly reading the paper together, for instance, before talking about your day. This will be complicated by the presence of children, so make sure you find space for the two of you (at least fifteen minutes) when you can catch up and chat about anything you want to with as little interruption as possible.

Pick a place you feel comfortable in

Never try to talk about anything of any importance if you are uncomfortable. Some couples make the mistake of attempting decisions, for example, during decorating or a busy time with kids. A conversation with your partner's legs while they are up a ladder or over a messy highchair with a yelling baby is not conducive to useful communication! Choose a room where you can be private (at least for a while) and sit down. Try to ensure your chairs are more or less level. If one is higher than the other, it can make the person in the lower seat feel inferior. Sit back and relax. Let your legs and arms rest loosely. Feeling at your ease will aid your thinking and talking. Tightly crossed arms and legs signal to your partner that you are defensive and anxious – not a good start to talking. Share a cup of tea, coffee, soft drink or a glass of wine (but be careful about alcohol as it can cause more problems than it solves). Or choose anything that allows you to feel comfortable and natural together.

Think about what you want to discuss

Reflecting on what you want to talk about is important. More trouble is caused in couple relationships by an off-the-cuff remark that hits like an Exocet missile at the heart of a partner. For example, launching into a complicated discussion about the credit card bill when you know your partner is sensitive to the issue without thinking what you really want to say can lead to heated arguments or long silences. Of course, you cannot spend all your time thinking through every remark in detail. You would soon start to sound unnatural. But it is important to think about what you want to say and how you want to express yourself. If the issue is serious, perhaps something to do with your work or children, it can help to make a few notes on what you have been thinking. This can also work if you are trying to decide what the right thing is to do in a particular situation. Divide a piece of paper in two, marking each side as either positive or negative. Mark in the columns things that are for or against your decision. Writing your thoughts down before talking, or assessing together what steps to take, can help your discussions lead to actions you feel are shared and that will succeed.

Talk to your partner sensitively

It's amazing how many couples seem to feel that living with someone means they can talk to them in a way that they would never do to their boss, mother or best friend. It is then easy to fall out when one or both of you feels disrespected or uncared for. Talking sensitively really means also listening sensitively. The golden rules for being sensitive are:

- Take responsibility for what you are saying – never use 'you make me feel …'. Instead say 'I feel …'. This has the double role of making you think what you really *do* feel and prevents your partner from raising his or her hackles in defence of an accusation.

- Observe the mood of your partner before starting to talk. If they seem tired or wound up, avoid conversations you know could lead to complicated outcomes. Pick a time when you can both be relaxed.

- Listen carefully to what your partner says in response to you. Switch off all your inner voices that shout assumptions, ideas you want to share or criticisms while your partner is speaking. Instead, be open to his or her remarks, even if you may want to disagree at some point in the future.

- Talk expressively, but do not shout or demand. Bullying your partner into an answer is not communicating.

- Slow down. Most couple conversations take place at top speed with the main aim of getting information relayed or decisions sorted as quickly as possible. Slowing down your delivery gives you time to make sense of what you are trying to say and your partner time to respond.

- Look your partner in the eye and maintain eye level during your conversations. Remove distractions such as newspapers (having a conversation with a disembodied voice from behind the morning paper is conversational suicide!), TV, radio or loud music. Do not wander around the room but try to sit opposite your partner so you can see each other easily.

- Let your partner know you are listening to them by reflecting back what they say. You can do this by summarising their remarks. For example, you might say after a discussion about a film you both saw 'So you are saying you thought the film was OK, but you didn't think much of Julia Roberts as a robot.' This helps your partner to know you have heard and understood what they are trying to say. It also leaves room for them to correct you if you have got the wrong end of the stick.

- Look for an ending to your talking and listening. This might mean saying 'Let's continue talking tomorrow' or 'I'm glad we talked about this' or 'I really enjoy hearing your ideas/opinions/thoughts'. At first, this might sound a bit forced, but it allows both of you to know where you stand at the end of a talk.

You can also apply these rules to briefer and less-important conversations such as who should take the kids to school or what you are going to eat for lunch. Here's a summary to help you make the best of all your communications.

Slow down what you want to say and give your partner time for a response.

Take responsibility for what you are saying.

Pick the right time and remove distractions.

Forget your assumptions about your partner.

Summarise what he/she has said to you so you know you have understood correctly.

Do not shout, demand or hector.

Listen carefully to what your partner is saying.

Create an ending so you both know where you stand.

Try These

Here are some games and ideas to help get you both talking easily and successfully. Now that you have a better idea of what helps make or break good talking, use the following tasks to encourage your conversations to improve:

1 Little and often is best for talking and listening. Ten to fifteen minutes of concentrated attention to each other, spread frequently throughout the day or the time available to you, is better than hours once a month. Long in-depth conversations often occur when something has gone wrong, are emotionally exhausting and usually fail to resolve issues. Sit down together and talk frequently. This will release tension and allow you to feel much closer to one another.

2 Choose some time when you can relax together – perhaps a lazy breakfast or a meal out – and talk about the following statements.

- I have a dream I have not fulfilled. True or false?
- In ten years' time I want to have . . .

- My perfect birthday would be . . .
- The first thing I remember about meeting you is . . .
- The three most important things about our relationship are . . .

Use these to get you started. Once you get the idea, you will find your own topics to discuss.

3 Ask your partner what their favourite piece of music, book or magazine, food, drink or journey is. (Pick just one to start with.) Then agree a time limit – about five to ten minutes – for your partner to explain their choice. Suggest they say why the item is appealing or interesting. When they have finished, do the same thing yourself. Carry on by picking other topics or stop when you feel you have said enough about one idea. The aim of this exercise is to allow you to learn more about your partner, but also to practise talking and listening to one another in a natural way. It is also good for preventing you from making assumptions. You may think you know what he or she likes, but are you right? And even if you were right, did you know the reasons for their choice? Allow yourself to occasionally be surprised – it's crucial in a relationship.

4 Think of a day you really enjoyed with your partner. This could be recent or some time ago. Tell them which day you have chosen and explain why it was important, interesting or just fun. Talk about what you did, how you felt towards them during the day and which elements of the day made things so good (for example, was it the weather, his or her behaviour, the venue and so on). Ask them to do the same for you. If you want to take things a bit further, talk about how you could replicate the occasion at another time.

5 Play a game of 'try out'. This is not an easy option so try some of the easier exercises above first. But if you want to fast

forward to thinking about some in-depth scenarios (useful if you feel your relationship is skating on the surface rather than offering a more profound partnership), this task could help you.

Ask your partner some of the questions below. Be aware that what you hear in response may be tough to get to grips with. Listen and respond carefully.

- What would you think we would do if you/I became pregnant and we were not planning a baby?
- If I/you lost my/your job, and we were in a financial mess, what do you think would be the best way forward?
- How do you think we would cope if one of us became disabled or chronically sick?
- Do you think I would turn to my parents, friends or you in a crisis? Why?
- What would you do if one of our children got into trouble with the police?
- If I had to move for my job, would you want to go with me?
- If one of us had an affair, how would we cope? Should we stay together or part? Why?

These are difficult questions. Most couples face them when the actual events have happened. Some survive and manage the best they can. But others do not. Testing out your feelings and responses to work out what you would do in a tricky situation is helpful because it can help you learn how to communicate even when the chips are down. You may never encounter the actual events, but you will have a better idea of how to survive a problem by talking about these subjects. Use the questions as jumping-off points rather than just as straight Q & A. Talk around the issues, volunteer your shared and different opinions and thoughts and practise handling difficult topics of conversation.

This is the first chapter in this book for a good reason. Communication is the cornerstone of any secure and successful relationship. All the subjects in the chapters that follow depend upon your ability to talk and listen with sensitivity, honesty and reliability. Practise the suggestions above and your relationship will feel more intimate and caring. If you run into trouble with your attempts to talk more freely, perhaps because you have argued, read the next chapter – it will help you resolve rows and communication difficulties.

2

STOP TRYING TO COME OUT ON TOP WHEN YOU ARGUE

Every couple has disagreements. It's normal to differ on views, opinions and ideas. In fact, differences of opinion demonstrate that your relationship has life and passion. The crucial issue for the health of your relationship is the style of how you let your partner know that you disagree with them and how you manage the fallout from arguments.

Arguments have a role to play in every relationship. They signal worry or fear about important issues that may have been missed in the rush of everyday life. They let your partner know how serious you are about something important. They can also be a jumping-off point for discussion about topics that need urgent attention. But if you argue and fight every day, find that every row is a competition to see who can come out on top or feel worn down by constant sniping and bickering, you have moved from healthy to unhealthy arguing.

There are basically two types of arguing: the first is healthy and can act as a catalyst to action; the second is unhealthy and is usually destructive.

Healthy arguing

Here's what healthy arguing looks like. Can you identify with it?

- Your rows never contain violence or aggression.
- Your arguments are contained – that is, they do not last for days and are usually cleared up in one day or less.
- Even in the middle of disagreeing, you still try to put yourself in his/her shoes to see things from his/her point of view.
- You do not try to belittle your partner or make them feel inadequate.
- When the dust has settled after a row, you say sorry for any hurt you have caused.
- You resolve to sort out what you have argued over. For instance, if you have argued over where to spend Christmas this year, you sit down afterwards and talk the issue through.
- You take action that prevents the row from being repeated in the future. For example, you decide where you want to spend Christmas this year and decide a strategy for some of the Christmases ahead.
- You do not drag up the same issues next time you argue.
- You forgive your partner for any hurt they have caused and try to learn from the experience.

Unhealthy arguing

This is what characterises unhealthy arguments. Have you had any experience of these?

- Your rows sometimes contain aggression or bullying.
- Your arguments drag on – sometimes for days or weeks. Small frustrations can spark full-scale rows because the issues from previous arguments do not get cleared up.
- You find it hard to see things from your partner's point of view. You also feel that he/she makes very little effort to understand your point of view.

- You often try to score points against your partner. For instance, if you argue about his/her inability to hold down a job, you will point out that you have never had the same trouble because you are not lazy.

- The argument is circular. You may start off fighting about one thing, go to another source of discomfort only to return to the original problem, without resolving anything. You may also find that you start arguing on something trivial, only to find you are arguing about the same topic you always argue about – money, sex, kids, work and so on.

- Trying to find a resolution frequently seems impossible. You struggle to move forward from arguments and often feel nothing changes.

- You frequently make assumptions about what your partner is feeling and thinking without checking out if they are correct.

- You hardly ever say sorry after a row. One, or both of you, may maintain long silences after an argument.

- You and/or your partner seem to find it hard to appreciate the hurt that has been caused.

The difference between these two approaches is that in the first, healthy, approach the couple has a bedrock of respect between them that may be dented by an argument, but not fatally cracked. In the second, unhealthy, approach the couple has lost the sense of what the disagreement might mean to the other person. They have allowed themselves to focus only on their own feelings and thoughts, without wondering what effect their unkind remark or bullying is having on their partner. It is this key difference that can make rows seem a manageable part of a satisfying relationship or a problem that never goes away, gradually eroding the joy in a partnership.

Five steps to resolving persistent arguments

If you have recognised some of the factors for unhealthy arguing in the lists above, then here are some ways to prevent dramas becoming a crisis.

Step One – Sort out the underlying problems to your rows

If you find you start off arguing about who should weed the garden, clean the car or collect the kids from Brownies but always end up arguing about money or sex, for instance, you need to sort out the underlying problem. If you fight about money, try to analyse what needs sorting out. If the bills never get paid because you think your partner ought to handle it or you disagree on spending priorities, you need to deal with these first. Put some time aside when you can be private and uninterrupted, get out a pad of paper and pen and write down the problem at the top of the page. Now brainstorm ways of resolving the issue. Write anything down, however wacky, and then pick out one or two solutions you might agree on. For instance, if she never pays the bills on time, consider trading tasks (he pays the bills, she cleans the car) or use direct debit so you can forget the problem. Be creative and open to new ways of approaching contentious topics.

Step Two – Take the heat out

The chief problem with arguments is the potential to hurt. Shouting or name-calling can be hard to recover from and has the potential to leave deep scars, especially if the argument is repeated. Remaining calm and controlled is better than blame and recrimination. You do not have to turn into an unemotional robot. You can stress your point, even raise your voice or say what you mean very firmly. What definitely does not help is having a go at your partner by belittling them with cruel or sarcastic comments. It may feel good to wound them, but it will never end in a sensible resolution. As Winston Churchill said, 'Jaw, jaw, jaw is better than war, war, war'. Remain calm by thinking carefully about what you really want to say. Pause in your replies and slow down the speed of what you are saying. Try reflecting back what your partner is saying. For example, if they say 'I am really fed up that you never put petrol in the car', reply by saying 'You're fed up because I never put petrol in the car'. (Use this technique sparingly because you can sound like a broken record, but in the early stages of a tiff it helps because your partner will know you have listened to her/him.)

Try to sit down and ask your partner to sit down. Look at them and allow yourself to listen to what they are saying. You are likely to feel you want to jump in with comments, usually to defend yourself, but avoid this. Instead, ask them why they feel angry and what you can do to help them. Attempt to get under the argument topic to the feelings the two of you are sharing. Think about whether the row has occurred – perhaps because you are tired, stressed or worried, for example. If you think it is happening because you are worn out from a long day at work, for instance, suggest you talk about the issue when you are both more relaxed.

Step Three – Who are you really arguing with?

Many of the arguments couples have are not with each other. They are with their mother and father, brothers and sisters, school friends and work mates. It may only take something small to trigger feelings of inadequacy, embarrassment and fear. Perhaps you were teased at school about your weight or hair colour. If your partner makes a casual comment about your figure or hair, you may prepare mentally to take your place behind the barricades. In reply, you are likely to snap out a response or spit out a remark that will touch some sensitive area in them. These ghosts of humiliations long gone often haunt couple relationships, so your partner may not know where the angry response you gave came from.

It can help to try to figure out what your 'sore spots' are. Do this by yourself. Writing things down can help, but you can do this just by thinking things through. Ask yourself what you know often upsets you. Hot topics are often body image and looks, intelligence and achievements, the ability to carry out domestic tasks (such as cooking or map reading) and self-esteem in general. If you have been put down in one of these areas, you may be super-sensitive to your partner criticising something in one of these areas. It could help to explain how painful it is to hear anything about these subjects so your partner understands your feelings. (If you feel you couldn't do this because your partner would take advantage of it, you have some serious problems that need working on, as the trust in your relationship is poor.) If you have outstanding issues with family members, it could help to try to sort these out, although this may not always be possible. If you want to talk it through with someone impartial, consider counselling. Find a therapist through the British Association of Counsellors and Psychotherapists www.bacp. co.uk or The British Association of Sexual and Relationship Therapists at www.basrt.org.uk

Step Four – Stop blaming

Most rows include the hurling of a considerable amount of blame. It is a safe bet that you will have told your partner at least once 'It's your fault' or 'It's not my fault' during a row. We do this because most of us learnt in childhood that to be held responsible for a difficulty was emotionally uncomfortable. We might have felt alienated by others or out of favour with our parents. This has the unconscious result that we fear abandonment. So during arguments, and even though an adult, you try to deflect blame at all costs. But blaming your partner as a way of achieving this end is likely to blow up in your face because they will want to avoid your blame bullet as well. They will throw recriminations back at you, with the inevitable result that one of you could spend a cold and uncomfortable night on the sofa.

You can get out of the blame culture in arguments by not pinning blame on your partner. When an argument starts think carefully about your own sense of responsibility. For instance, did you really promise to cut the grass, but now it's two feet tall? If your partner made a promise they have broken, are there important reasons why this has happened? It's also easy to assume that because *you* wanted something to happen, so did your partner. They may have avoided doing this – booking the tickets for an action or romance film you want to see, for instance – because they did not agree with your decision in the first place. So it is important to check out where the responsibility really lies – is it with you for making an assumption about your partner or with them for finding it hard to tell you what they really feel? Chances are it is partly with both of you. Thinking through the issues behind your desire to hold your partner totally responsible for a problem in this way helps to disarm blame. Disagreements will immediately begin to be less acrimonious and upsetting.

Step 5 – Always apologise and make amends for anything you got wrong

Do you believe that apologising makes you look weak? Or that you never get things wrong so what is there to apologise about? In fact, apologising after a row (or even during a row) can immediately help to stop you trying to come out on top at all costs. If you know you have hurt your partner it is important to acknowledge that you have done this and apologise. Even if you cannot agree with his/her point of view, saying sorry for hurts you caused during the row can open the way for both of you to begin to talk about how to resolve the problem issue.

There are better ways to apologise than others. Saying sorry means three important things:

- You must mean it. Insincere apology, grudgingly given, is worse than saying nothing.

- Apply it to the specific problem. For example, say 'I am sorry I hurt your feelings about the new coat you bought'. A general 'sorry' leaves your partner none the wiser about what you are apologising for.

- Take action to ensure the issue is sorted. The best part of an apology is not the words but the actions. Anyone can say sorry but it shows commitment and concern if you follow it up by never doing the same thing again or putting right something you spoilt. For instance, if you upset your partner by being rude to a friend of his/hers, make sure you do not do this again. (You might even need to apologise to the friend.)

How to have a good row

The title of this section probably sounds a bit odd. How can you have a good row? Surely a happy relationship would have two people living in harmony without a cross word? The truth is that if you lived in a relationship that was unruffled by life it would mean one of two things (or both). Firstly, that you are so bored you can't be bothered to disagree and, secondly, that you are denying and repressing your feelings in order to maintain a life without strife. Like the swan, you may look serene as you sail along but beneath the surface your legs are paddling very fast indeed. Disagreement (but not bullying or aggression) means that you have enough interest in one another to fall out occasionally and that you are not denying your natural feelings in order to maintain the illusion of the perfect couple.

So you might as well accept that all couples argue. Some couples do it by shouting, bickering and nagging. Still others do it by exchanging looks that could kill and days of not speaking at all. Take a look at the multiple choice below and mark those elements that seem to be present in your arguments. Then read the advice that could help you improve your personal style so that arguments are resolved and achieve something positive.

1

A) Your rows tend to blow up very quickly.

B) Your rows can last a long time, but you may not have shouting matches.

C) You say 'no, nothing's wrong' (even if there is) if your partner notices you are in a bad mood.

2

A) You shout a lot and you and/or your partner may indulge in storming out of the room.

B) You feel impelled to keep returning to the issue, demanding an answer from your partner.

C) You often find yourself hoping your partner will realise you have a grievance without having to say it out loud.

3

A) You say things you almost immediately regret.

B) You brood on what to say and choose the moment to say it that will make the most impact, knowing what will hurt most.

C) You may snap at each other, but quickly avoid other angry exchanges. However, the hurt is still real.

4

A) You do not have lots of arguments, but when you do they are humdingers.

B) You feel as if you argue a lot at a low level.

C) Sometimes, it feels as if one argument blends into the next one.

5

A) You do apologise but the hurt of the row can go on for days.

B) You may not apologise because the row never really feels closed.

C) It's hard to apologise for something that is never really given a voice.

6

A) You can have long gaps between arguments. However, you often notice minor irritations you do not share at the time.

B) You have spats most days, but they rarely develop into full-blown arguments.

C) You sometimes forget what you are fed up about as disagreements can blur into each other.

Mostly As

You are **volcanic arguers**. You store up issues of contention until one or both of you can hold them no longer. Then everything comes out in a huge head of steam. You shout and bluster, slam doors and threaten to split up. But you usually calm down fairly quickly (hours or, at most, a day or two) and regret sounding off in quite such a vitriolic manner. You may both try to laugh off the event, but can secretly feel hurt for a long period of time because you wonder if your partner really meant what he/she said to you in the heat of the row.

Have a better row

The main problem with volcanic arguers is that they try to keep a lid on minor issues for far too long. The best way to prevent this situation is to let off a little steam at regular intervals. Instead of sitting on annoyances for weeks, talk the issue through at the time it appears. For example, if you find you are sick of the washing-up sitting in the kitchen when you had expected your partner to clear it up, do not wait until the umpteenth occasion to shout your disappointment. Explain in a straightforward way why you thought he/she had agreed to clear it up at the time. Do this in a calm manner, avoiding sarcasm or complaints that you are tired of asking. You may need to say why the thing you are asking for, or complaining about, is important to you. For example, you may loathe the sight of the washing-up in the kitchen as you walk in from a long day at work or a stressful commute. Sharing your feelings can help your partner to see things from your point of view. Demanding a job be undertaken without explanation inevitably ends up with your partner feeling defensive. If you have an argument that demands an apology, make sure you do this in a way that helps your partner feel the apology is real. Do not try to make a joke of things or say 'you know how sorry I am'. Say why you are apologising, explaining what you regret. Lastly, look for ways to develop a positive outcome after a row. For instance, if you are fed up with the washing-up in the kitchen sink, could you afford a dishwasher? Or draw up a rota of who does what around the house.

Mostly **B**s

You are **long haul arguers.** Your preferred style of arguing is to bicker and pick at one another in order to let each other know over a long period of time that you are annoyed. Strangely, you may both feel that you know all too well when your partner is irritated, but have little idea what they are actually miffed about. Both of you know exactly where your partner's 'chink in the armour' is and are experts at poking it with your sharp tongue. But all this needling of each other rarely results in a change in attitude. Indeed, the sarcastic remarks of your partner may now sound like so much background noise that you have almost learnt to ignore them. Almost, but not quite. Beneath what looks like your acceptance of the situation, there is often a deep lake of resentment just waiting to burst its banks. Couples who bicker for years are often taken by surprise when one partner either votes with his/her feet and leaves or becomes a **volcanic** arguer as years of pent-up feeling comes to the surface.

Have a better row

The problem with bickering is that it is like water dropping on a stone – eventually it may make a difference but it will take a long time to do it. It also acts like a smokescreen. You may be hiding behind bickering because it allows your partner to know there is something wrong without the responsibility of having to face resolving it. To break bickering and sniping you must tackle the root of the problem. Sit down with a hot drink and ask your partner to list the top five issues that you tend to disagree about. (Only attempt this when you are NOT in the middle of a row.) Once you have both put your lists on the table, discuss why the topics you have chosen might be hot potatoes. For example, if one of your topics is the division of housework, think through why this might be the case. Ask yourself some key questions. Is it linked to stretched and busy lifestyles? Or could it be a set of assumptions that you have brought from a former relationship or your family home? (For example, 'Dad always washed the car so I expected you to do the same'.) If you realise you have dragged a set of assumptions with you from a previous situation, talk about why this has happened and seek a solution that fits the two of you, not your family or a former relationship.

Do you criticise instead of praise? This habit can cause continual bickering because couples stop noticing the good things their partner does. This can be emotionally exhausting, causing a relationship to feel as if it is dreary and tiring instead of enlivening and support-ive. Every day, look for two things that you can praise or say thank you for in your partner. These do not have to be big events. Say 'I appreciate you bathing the baby' or 'Thanks for a tasty dinner'. Acknowledge when they look tired or worried – try 'I can see you've had a hard day', for example. You may not completely stop griping at first, but gradually your desire to criticise will diminish. You should also notice a lift in the mood of your relationship. You will feel lighter and more able to manage day-to-day irritations without blame. It's important that you both agree to do this or it will feel as if one of you is putting lots of effort in while the other just mops it up like a sponge. Essentially, bickering is a form of avoidance. If you can face the impor-tant issues head on, and tackle them, the bickering will stop.

Mostly **C**s

You are **meaningful silence arguers.** You are very unlikely to give vent to your deep feelings and may tell other people that you 'never have a cross word', but you communicate displeasure in other ways. You know when your partner disapproves of you because they sigh deeply, do not speak to you, refuse to touch you (they may even decide to sleep in the spare bed or on the couch to give you the message) or communicate through others – even via your children. Why do you choose this method? Because it allows you to tell your partner how hurt or cross you are without you needing to use language. Communication when you are angry is fraught with difficulties. The high emotions of arguing can cause you to let slip the very thoughts you have been trying to keep hidden. Remaining silent is like arguing with a safety net – you never have to take the risk of saying the wrong thing.

Have a good row

It's possible you have adopted this method because you have wit-nessed the effects of out and out anger in your parental family or with another partner. You may have been left with a fear that if you say something even slightly out of line, things could get out of control. So you try to communicate it in a way that is obvious but leaves you less open to confrontation. The problem with your silent method is that it leaves you wide open to misinterpretation. If you both keep this up throughout your relationship you will have no hope of knowing what the problem is, why it has occurred and how you will resolve it.

The other reason couples find themselves in this mode of disagreeing is because they subscribe to the 'If you loved me you would know what the problem is. If you do not know what is troubling me you do not really love me' myth. This type of arguing often occurs in couples who are still developing their relationship, perhaps in the early months or years. They may be afraid to test the other out in the way that couples who feel completely secure together are not. This style is also manipulative. It pulls on the guilty heartstrings of your partner, asking them to take pity on you, or to try to win you back, rather than making an honest appraisal of what the difficulty really is.

The first step you need to take as a **meaningful silence arguer** is to break the silence. Next time you notice tension in the air, take a deep breath and say 'I feel that there is something wrong. Shall we talk about it?'. Use 'I feel . . .' to start your sentences as this helps you to say what you are feeling and puts your partner off the defensive. It might help to suggest a topic if you feel reasonably confident that the problem is linked to this. For example, 'I wonder if you are upset because I forgot to buy milk on the way home tonight?' Be tentative so that if your partner does not agree, they have space to say this without feeling under attack. Be patient, and leave room for both of you to think about what you want to say. You may find it tough at first, but practise this reflective style of observation and you will soon find it easier to talk about problems. You will know you are improving when you are able to disagree openly without fearing the consequences.

Special problems

For most people arguments do not always carry the threat of violence and aggression, although most couples can recall moments when they came close to this. Because we are human beings arguing brings with it ancient instincts about winning and fighting for survival. We may be more sophisticated and socialised than our primitive ancestors, but we can still feel extremely strong emotions if we perceive a threat. In some situations this can lead to violence and aggression in a relationship.

All violence is born out of fear. This may not seem clear if you are on the end of a clenched fist or hateful behaviour. You could be forgiven for thinking that it is you who are afraid, not your aggressor. But your aggressor is afraid. They are afraid that you will do the thing they do not want you to do – leave, stand up for yourself or enlist others to help you. So they threaten, or actually carry out, violence towards you. Violence is all about control. They want to control you in order to prevent you from taking your own decisions. They are terrified about being unable to control life so they seek to control everything in their environment, and, as their partner, that includes you.

Patterns of violence and aggression

If you asked the average person on the street if they would stay with a violent partner they would probably say 'no way'. But many people do stay with someone who is violent, often for years. Police records show that women (and some men) with a violent partner often tolerate years of abuse before taking the step to leave. So what keeps a person with a violent partner?

The most common pattern is the **circle of violence**.

1 The non-violent partner realises that tension is rising in the relationship. He/she may not know how to deal with this, or fears raising the issue because it has always resulted in problems in the past. She/he may try to keep the situation calm by being especially wary of doing or saying anything that could cause trouble. Common responses are to try to avoid contact with a partner or keeping children away from a partner.

2 An insignificant event occurs. Perhaps something around the home sparks an angry response in the partner. An argument ensues, during which a violent event occurs. A variation on this scenario is that the violent partner feels a build-up of anger within them and takes this out on an unsuspecting partner without any disagreement being evident.

3 The partner who has perpetuated the violence appears to be remorseful. They may promise never to do the same again and even be especially affectionate and interested in their partner. Their partner wants to believe that this is the person they really love. (This can happen against all the evidence. Their partner may have done this several times before, but they still hang on to their hope that the kinder and attentive side of their partner will prevail.)

4 There may then be a period of calm. This can feel as if the relationship is back on track. But before long the tension begins to rise and the couple go back to Phase One again. The circle is complete.

This circle can be made much worse by alcohol or drug abuse or mental health problems. If you recognise this circle in your own relationship, here are some things you can do. You should bear in mind that if this circle has become entrenched over several years, the likelihood of your partner seeing the light and changing overnight is very small.

- *Your love is not enough.* It is wrong to hope that your love alone will prevent his/her violence towards you. Your perception of what is happening will also be affected by the way in which the violence destroys your self-esteem. Try keeping a private diary. Record your thoughts, feelings and events over a period of a few weeks. Reading it back could help you to see what is really going on without the mental screening that repeated aggression can cause. For example, you may find yourself thinking 'It won't happen again', 'I'll change to prevent him/her getting angry', 'I know he/she really loves me', etc. Reading your diary could help you see things as they really are.

- *If aggression and/or violence looks imminent, put physical space between you and the instigator.* Leave the room or house. Do not wait for the situation to worsen in the hope you can control him/her.

- *Draw a line in the sand.* Make it clear you will not tolerate his/her violence. Say exactly what you will do if he/she carries out their threats. And then carry out your promise if the aggression is repeated. Never threaten violence in response to his/her threats. Insist he or she gets help with their anger problem.

- *Get help.* Talk to your GP, social worker, local police, work support services or anyone you trust to help you deal with the situation. Never try to cover up his/her actions. They are a crime and should be dealt with as such.

The ultimate outcome of all arguments should be to find win/win solutions. This is so that, as partners, you have a resolution that allows for both of you to have at least some of what you want. This is healthy arguing. If you regularly feel you cannot express yourself, or that your arguments are all sound and fury but no resolution, you are caught in a net of unhealthy arguments. Taking some time to develop better ways of managing rows could improve your whole relationship.

The next chapter looks at affection – why it is important and how to boost it with your partner. Maintaining a high level of affection can prevent rows ever happening in the first place. Take a look at the next chapter to find new ways of feeling closer and secure in your relationship.

3

SHARE AFFECTION
EVERY DAY

If you were asked in a survey what the most important thing in your relationship was, what would you say? You might suggest commitment, trust and a sense of a shared future. But there is a strong argument for something else to come top of the list – something that lots of couples take for granted in their relationship – affection. In fact, a recent Reader's Digest survey found that 22 per cent of men wanted their partners to be more affectionate, while 17 per cent of women wished they could talk more openly to their partner about intimacy. This overlooked element of couple relationships is crucial in maintaining a close partnership. You may not notice it if you have it every day, but you will soon notice if affection is absent. The giving and receiving of affection can help any relationship feel more secure and increases the chance of a strong and enduring bond.

Why affection is important

From the moment you are born you respond to touch. Skin-to-skin contact, from the hands of your parents and carers, from the warmth of your mother's breast and the stroking and cuddling you are given as you develop, will help you to thrive. Babies who do not receive regular, comforting and loving touch are likely to weigh less and develop more slowly. Parents also instinctively speak to their baby in a special way. They tend to use a tone of voice that is in a higher pitch than normal and repeat and reflect their baby's babbling as they learn to talk. As we grow up we associate caressing, stroking and cuddling with acceptance and love. If we are denied warmth and affection, we associate it with rejection. As we grow through childhood into teenage we may feel embarrassed if our parents show too much overt affection in front of our friends, but we still need affection. Sensitive parents learn the right moment to display affection. Later still, as we learn about relationships, affection becomes a tool for telling the person we care for how we feel about them.

It is important to understand that affection is not full-on sex! It is possible to have some of the attributes of affection in sex (more about this later), and sharing affection can improve sex, but affection should be part of a loving relationship without it always becoming sexual. In adult relationships, affection might more accurately be described as sensual rather than sexual. Affection is like oil that helps machinery to perform well. If you have it, you will help your relationship to run smoothly. Affection also has an important bonding role. Chimpanzees, who share 95 per cent of our DNA and, from an evolutionary point of view, are our nearest cousins, spend hours each day grooming one another in groups. This constant touching confirms their place in the group and gives a sense of belonging. Experiments show that baby monkeys only thrive when they are in regular contact with their mothers, even if they are fed and cared for in other ways.

Although we might consider ourselves a long way up the evolutionary tree from monkeys and chimps, we still need regular touching, praise and support to help us feel cared for. Children and adults who are not shown this kind of care can feel cut off and out of touch with others. This is especially true in couple relationships. If your partner hardly ever shows you affection or never tells you how much you mean to them, how can you know what they feel? You might argue with this by saying 'I work hard and keep the family financially afloat – that's my way of saying how much I care' or 'I cook his/her meal everyday – he/she must know how I feel'. But nothing says 'I love you' other than 'I love you'! Cooking or working, for example, could mean 'I like you' or 'This is my duty' or even 'Come to bed'. Of course, if you say 'I love you' you should mean it, but the main concern for lots of couples is that it is never said or demonstrated at all. The chief problem is that lots of people find it hard to express themselves in an affectionate way.

Common blocks to expressing feelings

- **'I'm not used to it. My parents and family never showed their feelings to me and I feel awkward if I am expected to.'**

It is true that how you are brought up influences the way in which you show your feelings. If you are naturally reserved, it is not possible to turn you into a touchy-feely person overnight, and it may not even be a good idea to try to alter your character in such a total way. But if you are living with someone who you care about, you might find it helps you both to feel closer and more intimate if you can at least occasionally put an arm around your partner or say how much he or she means to you. Even small gestures of affection can create a feeling that you are both cared for.

- **'It's a show of weakness to be all soppy. My partner would always be expecting me to let them have their own way.'**

Why should your relationship be a competition? If you feel this way, it might be because you were brought up in a family where you had to compete for your parents' attention. In an effort to avoid the pain of struggling to be good enough, or intelligent enough, to be noticed you may have decided never to engage with that kind of behaviour again. You may reason to yourself that if your partner doesn't know what they mean to you by now it is too late to do anything about it. To counter this view, you could try an experiment. Spend a week being a bit more affectionate – kiss or cuddle a couple of times a day. Then ask your partner if they noticed a difference and what they thought of it. It's a good bet that they will say they enjoyed the attention and you may learn that being affectionate doesn't need to be frightening.

- '**I think we show enough feelings in this family. The kids are always shouting, my partner is always telling me what he/she thinks and I often feel exhausted by all the emotion washing about.**'

If your family and relationship are on the melodramatic side, the idea that you should show more feeling can seem a bit daunting. But being affectionate can have a calming effect on an over-wrought situation. Take some time to sit quietly together and hold hands or snuggle up together. It might help not to say anything and just allow yourself to enjoy the intimacy. Try choosing a time of day when you can say 'this is our time' to indulge in a bit of quiet cuddling.

- '**I'm an affectionate person but my partner is not. I would like them to be more loving towards me but they do not seem to have it in them.**'

This is a very common phenomenon. One partner gives out a lot of affection, but receives very little. This can lead to a kind of 'affection burn-out' when the affectionate partner just gives up because they are worn out with giving out. Strangely, this kind of situation can arise because the more affectionate partner never voices their needs. They may expect their partner to understand what they are asking for by mind reading. Next time you feel let down that your hug was not returned as you hoped, try saying 'I would really love you to cuddle me' or 'I really like it when we kiss goodbye/hello'. Regularly offering feedback in this way can have a surprising outcome. You may have to do it for a few weeks, but as your partner gets more used to what you want they will gradually begin to respond. If they do not respond, they may be holding out because they want some kind of power and control over you (see below).

Some other blocks to affection

Anger

If you feel angry, it will be hard to show and receive affection. After the dust has settled, saying sorry and offering a hug can help you both feel better about things. If you suffer from chronic anger (that is, there is a low level of animosity all the time), affection will be difficult. Before you start to try to be more affectionate, try to understand why you feel so irritated with each other and deal with the source of your annoyance (see Chapter Two).

Anxiety

Worry and stress can prevent you from reaching out to your partner and stop them offering you affection. If you know what you are worrying about, and that it will pass (for example, a short-term financial problem), your affection levels should improve once it has passed. If you find you are stuck in the groove of worry, perhaps because one of you is ill, it is very important to keep up loving contact. A gentle squeeze of the hand or a kiss on the forehead can be very reassuring and say more than lots of explanations about how you feel.

Power and control

Some couples use affection as a weapon. They may try to get their own way by rewarding their partner with affection when he/she does what they want. Others withdraw, becoming cold and unresponsive in order to draw attention to some issue they feel has been overlooked. This is natural in most couple relationships, and tolerable if it is happening a small percentage of the time. But if you keep doing it, your relationship is based on manipulation rather than mutual respect. Essentially, you have suffered a communication breakdown. You are not talking openly so you are communicating in code. The trouble with this approach is that code is difficult to read and means different things to different people. If you want to boost affection, you need to talk about what you want, not use affection, or the lack of it, to achieve what you want.

Embarrassment

Some people just feel awkward showing their feelings. This can be due to lack of practice or worries that he/she will read the moment inaccurately or say the wrong thing. The key question to ask is – what do I feel embarrassed about? Is it that I might be misinterpreted? Or that my cuddle technique is somehow lacking? The answer to this question is to match actions to words. Put your arms loosely around your partner and say 'You're great', 'I'm proud of you', 'Thank you', or whatever seems to suit the situation. In this way your partner will know what your affectionate gesture means to you and how it is intended for them. Embarrassment often comes from a lack of confidence about how your partner will respond. Saying why you are doing what you are gives them information about what is going on, allowing them to respond to you. After a few weeks, you should find that your day-to-day communication also improves, as this habit of saying what you are feeling is infectious, helping you to feel closer and more loving to each other.

Ways to boost affection in everyday life

So now you are convinced that affection is good for relationships (research shows that regular and shared affection increases the chance of a relationship lasting) how can you increase it in your daily life?

Here are some simple ways to increase shared affection:

1   **Make time to say hello and goodbye to one another**. In a busy life, it is easy to dash out of the door shouting 'good-bye' as you throw your coat on. But if you can spare twenty seconds to say goodbye face to face, even with a kiss, it will give you a lift all day. The same goes for a proper 'hello'. It might be tempting for both of you to get home and race straight into sorting out the kids or opening the post. But if you take a few minutes to say 'hello', have a hug or just a brief conversation about the day, you will feel eased back into the relationship rather than passing each other on parallel tracks.

2   **Write it down**. You may not be a budding Shakespeare, but a simple note stuck on the fridge or in a wallet that says 'I care about you and will be thinking of you today' improves intimacy and gives a real sense of belonging. If you need an excuse, pick Valentine's Day, birthdays, anniversaries or Christmas to write your personal message. But any day will do!

3   **Make it part of daily life**. Next time you make him/her a cup of tea, bend down and give him/her a kiss. Cuddle up last thing as you prepare to sleep and hold hands as you stroll along. Regular brief acts of affection are as good as long sessions of passion to improve the bond in your relationship. This method of improving affection is especially good if you

feel awkward in showing affection. Brief affectionate acts will help you to get used to showing your feelings in this way, allowing you to build confidence in giving and receiving affection.

4   **Give a small gift**. Giving your partner a small surprise gift can remind you both of how you felt when you first met. A bar of his/her favourite chocolate, tickets to a film or cooking his/her favourite meal says 'You are important to me'. Avoid the big all-star present (even if you can afford it) as this can feel overwhelming and make your partner feel uncomfortable, especially if they think they have to return your largesse. Small, quirky or sentimental presents suggest you have thought about them during the day. Think of something that has meaning from your early days together – hire a video of a film you enjoyed or learn to cook a dish you first shared.

5   **Add it to sex**. It is surprising how many couples forget to use affection as part of sex, especially the spoken exchange of feeling. Perhaps this is because we have become more interested in sexual technique than feelings, but affection in sex can enhance sensual and erotic feelings. Whisper 'I love you' or 'Your body really turns me on' and watch the positive effect it has on your partner. Signs of love, genuinely expressed, during love making can improve responsiveness and sexual satisfaction for both partners.

6   **Use it when you say sorry**. If you have had an argument and want to say sorry, showing affection and warmth will make the apology what you really want – heartfelt and honest. Try taking your partner's hand across the table and saying 'I'm sorry about the row' or 'I'm sorry I forgot to meet you from work', for example. Avoid a dramatic show of

feeling or a huge bunch of roses. Test out the ground by offering a hand to hold or a light touch on the shoulder. This will allow your partner to reach out to you rather than feel blackmailed into making up when they may still be tussling with their emotions after a fall-out.

7   **Share it in adversity**. A hug or a few kind words when you have bad news, are trying to cope with a tricky situation, or if your partner is upset helps difficult times seem easier. A gentle arm on the shoulder or a quiet 'It's OK, we'll get through this together' will help you and your partner to feel you are facing a problem together rather than struggling alone. In this situation, touch can often say more than a thousand words and be a great comfort. If you do not know what to say (often the case if you are shocked or upset) a cuddle can tell your partner you are on their side.

8   **Use it to enhance a celebration**. If you are celebrating – perhaps a birthday or a job promotion – give your partner a hug and tell them how proud you are of them. It's surprising how little people praise each other. Celebrations will seem all the better if you share your pleasure through touch and thoughtful words. If you are giving an anniversary or birthday card, write some loving words to go alongside your usual 'Love from . . .'

9   **Share it to give a sense of peace**. Touch can stop a baby from crying or soothe a restless toddler. It's the same with adults. Find some quiet time when you can spend half an hour cuddled up together. Listen to some gentle music or simply revel in being quiet and still. There is no need to talk. Holding each other in this way is a luxury that lots of couples find difficult. They may think it should be a prelude to sex, or a waste of time in a busy day. As a stress reducer it

can be magical. You may need to practise as most people are not used to lying (or sitting) still for this length of time without talking. Do it a couple of times a week and you should notice it adding a sense of calm to your lives.

10 **Let it be part of your bond to one another**. Regular shared affection creates and maintains a bond in relationships. A little affection, shared every day, will quietly add to your sense of togetherness. It may not be dramatic in the way that sexual passion is, but in terms of your relationship it plays a more important role than sex.

If you shut affection out of your relationship it can be difficult to reintroduce. The less you touch, or say 'I love you', a downward spiral can develop. You will find it hard to be affectionate and your partner will also find it hard to say the words to you. Before you know where you are, neither of you knows how to be tender towards the other. Use the ideas above to prevent this ever happening and your relationship will be stronger. However, there are times when it is not a good idea to use affection.

When not to use affection

● **Never use it to get your own way.**

Using affection to manipulate your partner into doing what you want is unfair. For example, saying 'I love you and if you loved me too you would do what I wanted' is not true affection. It also means that next time you say it, they are not likely to believe you. Gradually your trust in one another is worn away so that any affection becomes a redundant emotional currency between you.

● **Never make a partner feel sorry for you.**

If you are in the middle of an argument, or even threatening to separate, saying 'But I love you' will kill negotiations stone dead.

This is a delaying tactic, produced in order to avoid dealing with the problem at hand. It is OK to say 'I am sorry and I love you' after a row, but it can be a smokescreen that stops real discussion from taking place.

● **Never use if you do not mean it.**

If your partner is asking for affection it can be tempting to give it back, no matter what you are feeling. You may want to avoid disappointing them or put off the evil day when you must be honest about your emotions. But if you do this, they will develop expectations of the relationship that cannot be fulfilled. Even if you know that being honest will hurt your partner, it is better to risk this than hide behind false affection or words of love that you do not mean.

● **Never use it if it will cause embarrassment.**

You may think your partner is a 'lovely bunny wunny', but saying this at the office party in front of his/her boss is a bad idea! Some forms of affection are private affairs better kept to private moments. Adjust your behaviour to your circumstances – a full-on snog with your partner might be OK in bed, but not in the queue at the local supermarket. Sometimes, embarrassing affection in front of others is territorial in nature. Your partner may be laying a claim to you. A passionate kiss or an arm tightly wrapped around your waist is a clear signal to others in the room: 'this person is mine'. It's more common at the start of a relationship when both of you may feel less secure about whether you will stay together. If it goes on once the relationship is more established, it is important to ask yourselves if you are as secure as you think you are. Your partner may be trying to convince himself or herself that the relationship is as steady as a rock rather than built on sand.

Speaking affectionately

If you are not used to speaking to your partner in an affection-ate way, or if you feel stuck in the same old ways of saying how you feel, here are some ideas to help you talk with affection to a partner. Use them as prompts rather than a script. If you use them word for word, your partner will think you are a machine rather than a flesh-and-blood lover!

- *Tell your partner how proud you are of them.* For instance, say how well they have done a job around the home, how pleased you are they are 'salesperson of the month', or that they man-aged to do something they find difficult. Try 'I'm really proud of the way you …'. Or 'It's really great you did so well at …'.

- *Tell them what they mean to you.* For example, say 'I couldn't have got through the last few months without your support' or 'It's so nice to spend the evenings with you'. Don't forget to say 'I love you' or 'You mean so much to me'. It can also be good to be specific as this helps your partner to know that not just anyone could meet your needs. Try 'When you smile at me I think I can do anything' or 'I was nervous about giving the speech at the wedding, but when I looked at you I knew I could do it'.

- *Reflect on what is happening.* Seize the moment to say some-thing affectionate. If you are really enjoying something – an evening out or a football match, for instance – say 'Having you here with me makes this so great' or 'This wouldn't be half so good without you'.

- *Say what you feel at difficult moments.* You may not think that difficult times are the best places to show affection, but affec-tion can help you and your partner to feel supported and loved when you most need it. For instance, try 'I know you are worried about your mother's health but I will help you get through it' or 'I realise we have argued about money a lot lately, but I still love you and want our relationship to work'.

- *Celebrate good times.* Telling your partner what you feel when things are going well can make a good time great. For example, try 'This holiday with you is the best I've ever had' or 'My birthday is so special because you are here to share it with me'.

Touching affectionately

You may wonder if you need to know how to touch affectionately. Surely everyone knows how to do this without instruction? While it is true that most people know how to give a hug or hold a hand, it can become a thorny issue in couple relationships. This is because some people fear that a demand for sex is actually what is being suggested by affectionate touching and shy away from it. Women seem to think this more often than men, but some men also find being touched difficult because they feel it is somehow 'weak' to receive a loving touch. This means that some couples avoid touching, other than during sex, because they are afraid that it will be misinterpreted. If you recognise this state of affairs, here is how to give and receive touch so that you get the warmth but not the problems that go with it.

- *Avoid the erogenous zones.* Touch your partner on any part of their body that is not chiefly associated with sex – usually the crotch and breasts. Some couples do find it comforting to touch these areas and can handle the ambivalence about sexuality and affection. But lots of couples feel that this muddies the water so that *any* touch is construed as an invitation to sexual activity. Sex can be tender, but tenderness without sex is also comforting and loving.

- *Hold hands.* This is probably the simplest touch there is. Try holding hands when you are out walking, watching TV, at the cinema or listening to music. Avoid gripping too tightly. Just rest your hands together, or entwine your fingers without exerting any squeezing.

- *Stroke the face.* The face is richly endowed with responsive nerve endings, but many couples ignore it when touching each other. Try gently tracing your partner's face with a finger, or placing both hands on either cheek as you kiss them. The nape of the neck and under the chin are also pleasant to touch and have caressed. Use the flat of your hand to stroke here. Not everybody likes having their hair stroked, but some people find it very relaxing. Lie with your head in your partner's lap and ask them to stroke (or gently brush) your hair.

- *Pat the shoulder or knee.* This kind of touching is useful if you are parting. A reassuring pat, or soft squeeze, on the shoulder says 'I'm thinking about you as we part'. A pat on the knee is also intimate, but not so much that you cannot do it in public.

- *Put your arms around shoulders or waist.* This kind of touching is quite difficult to maintain if you are moving, but it is possible to walk with your arms slung across each other's lower back. It can be useful if you want to talk as it keeps you level with each other and able to look at one another without too much difficulty.

- *Give a hug or cuddle.* A warm hug can say 'hello', 'goodbye' or 'I've missed you' and lots of other things that are unique to the two of you. Beware of squeezing too much (although a bear hug can be fun sometimes!). Lay your head against your partner's neck for a real feeling of intimacy or bury your head in his/her chest for a sense of closeness.

- *Share a snuggle.* This is really a lying-down cuddle! It is good in bed last thing at night. Try lying in the spoon position (he/she with his/her front to his/her back) and wrap your arm over your partner. Use the opportunity to whisper a loving goodnight before you drift off to sleep.

These are just a few ideas to get you started. You will already have some favourites or variations on the suggestions above. The important thing is that you practise them regularly so you build a store of ways of demonstrating affection. Once you get into the habit of giving and receiving affection you will probably wonder how you did without it. Affection is one of the key measures in couple relationships. If you lack it, your relationship may crack under pressure because you will have no way to express your feelings for one another. If you have it, your partnership will be the stronger for it. You will be able to tell one another how you feel and communicate without words when you need to.

4

HANG ON TO YOUR MEMORIES

Research that was carried out during the 1990s on couples in a psychological 'relationship laboratory' found something surprising. Alongside the expected findings on keeping communication alive and successful negotiation, long-term couples had an unusual attribute. They were found to be like elephants – they never forgot what brought them together. Couples who found it hard to remember why they had chosen the partner they were with or what had happened in the early part of their partnership were more likely to argue and split up. Those couples who could recall how they felt when they first set eyes on their lover, and shared events from long ago, were more likely to feel satisfied with their relationship.

Perhaps this is less surprising than it first appears. Laughing together at the bizarre fashions you wore as you look at the photo album, or a private recollection of a first kiss, gives you a shared history. This allows you to see yourselves as a couple who have survived previous ups and downs, giving confidence that you can survive anything the future can throw at you. If you cannot recall how you managed situations in the past, or revel in the first date you shared, maybe you do not really know how you will deal with celebrations or disasters in the future. Helping yourself to remember the progression of your relationship, it seems, is good for you.

?

How much can you remember?

Here is a fun quiz to help you remember what formed you as a couple. Write your answers down and ask your partner to award marks out of ten for accuracy. Ask him or her to do the quiz at the same time, sharing your answers when you are both finished. If neither of you can remember, spend a little time talking to see if you can jog your memory. The idea of the quiz is to make you smile not argue so if you quibble over the answers, put the quiz aside and talk more generally about how you met and your early time together. Remember that it is not a competition!

1 Where was your first meeting?

2 What was he/she wearing?

3 What were the first words you said to one another?

4 Did you know anything about each other before you met? What was it?

5 What was your first impression?

6 Where did you go for your first date? Can you name what you ate/film you saw/pub you went to, etc?

7 Where did you share your first kiss?

8 Name three things you really liked to do together on your following dates.

9 When did you first say 'I love you'?

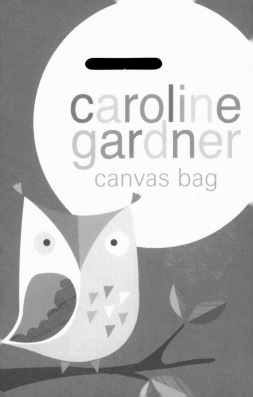

caroline gardner

canvas bag

carolinegardner.com

bgc007

5 034931 087231

made in china

10 Where did you first make love?

11 How long was it before you met his/her family?

12 Where were you both working when you met?

13 Describe three things about the places you both lived in when you first met.

14 Name two of his/her friends at the time.

15 What was your first argument about?

16 How did you make up?

17 What was the first thing you bought jointly?

18 Name a meal he/she cooked for you.

19 What was his/her favourite music at the time? Can you name a single by the artist?

20 What was the name of her favourite perfume or his favourite aftershave at the time?

If you can answer most of these you are doing very well indeed. If you get half or more, there are some gaps in your memory that you might need to work on. If most of them are a mystery, you may be trying to avoid remembering an unhappy start to your relationship. If you have trouble remembering things from the past (either short or long term), use your five senses to help you.

Seeing

What did things look like? Can you remember the colour of his shirt or her outfit when you first met? Draw a picture in your mind of the place you were at. Try to recall details like the colour of the paint on the wall or the signs around you. If you were in a pub or club, remember the flashing lights or colour of the clothes on friends who may have been with you. Think about the fashions of the time.

Hearing

Try to recall the sounds that you experienced on your first dates. What music was in the charts, and what did you play a lot at home or in the car? Work on remembering his/her voice at the time and the kind of things you talked about. Is there a sound that seems to sum up your early days? For instance, if you rode a motorbike, is it the sound of the engine, or birdsong as you walked in the park that reminds you of being together?

Touch

Try to remember not only the first time you touched each other or kissed (although these are important) but also the texture of the clothes you wore. If it was winter, were you wrapped up in thick coats and scarves? Or if it was summer, can you recall the breeze in your hair or cool water by the sea? Next, think about the way his/her skin felt and the texture of his/her hair.

Taste

What were your favourite meals at that time? Is there a flavour that brings him/her to mind? Concentrate on drinks you shared or special meals you might have had on an anniversary or birthday. Indulge yourself in the excitement of your first kiss or love making, allowing the taste of skin and lips to come to mind.

Scent

Perhaps the most evocative of the senses for the past. (If you doubt this, think about how the smell of a school – school dinners and chalk dust – can take you back to your school days in a second). Remember how he/she smelt – probably a mixture of their choice of perfume or aftershave at the time and their personal 'scent' that everyone has. Interestingly, recent research demonstrates that we are likely to be attracted to another by their pheromones. These are usually undetectable scents that make a man or woman sexually attractive. They seem to be based on how different their immune system is to our own. The more different, the more likely you are to find them attractive. This seems to help widen the tolerance to disease of any potential offspring, and is therefore good for the survival of our children, and their children, in the future.

Early days

Now that you have used your senses as an aid to remembering your early days together, think about what was important about those times. Did you immediately feel you had discovered your soul mate? Or was the relationship slower to take off? You may even have disliked each other at first. (Some relationships do start in this way, often because the potential partner 'hides' their true self in company or at work.) Ask yourself the following questions to help you get to grips with what the relationship was like when you first met.

Why did you fancy them?

A pretty basic question that some people answer by saying 'he/she had a cute bum'! But our attraction to someone is rarely as simple as the physical attributes we admire when we first meet him or her. It is important to feel sexually attracted to someone, although this can be lesser or greater, according to the initial relationship, but beyond the first date your partnership will be more than what you think about their body. So, what were the things you liked? Did they have a good sense of humour? Or were they the shy one you wanted to bring out of their shell? When we first meet someone aspects of ourselves that we unconsciously recognise in the other often attract us. This might seem a strange idea. After all, many couples often seem very different from each other when viewed from the outside. In fact, most couples share similar values and backgrounds as well as cultural and religious beliefs. Those that get together across religious, cultural and ethnic divides can sometimes struggle to make their relationship work. Hopefully, this will change as we enjoy greater diversity in society, but a core of shared values is often at the heart of what makes someone attractive or unattractive, even if you do not realise it at the time.

If it helps, make a list of all the things you know you found attractive and then ask yourself what some of the hidden attributes of your partner were. You might also find it helpful to reflect on whether they met a need in you. Lots of couples, unconsciously or consciously, found their relationships on what their partner can do for them. If this sounds a bit mercenary it is not meant to! It is a natural part of all human relationships. For example, if you are shy you might pick a partner who is outgoing and lively so they 'do' the socialising bit for you. In turn, they might have picked you for your ability to remain calm when they are excitable. This works for lots of people as each of them creates one half of a whole, allowing them to have experiences, with the support of their partner, that they may have avoided in the past, though it can present problems for some people. Imagine you are someone who relies on a partner to be strong in the face of adversity while you lean on his or her ability to cope. If they are suddenly ill or suffer a crisis of confidence, you may have few resources to draw on to manage the situation, causing meltdown in your relationship. So all couple relationships are a matter of balance. How much you depend on your partner and how much you do for yourself can be a difficult issue to tackle at the start of a relationship. Moving from dependence to independence, and vice versa, happens thousands of times over the life of the average couple. The way you handle this can be crucial in sustaining your relationship.

What kept you in the relationship?

Once you have met someone the next phase is to keep the relationship going while you both explore what you mean to each other. Some relationships founder almost immediately. Perhaps the attraction was pure lust rather than long-term interest, or some weeks on you discover you have little in common. But if you stick around for a while, something is keeping you interested. It is helpful to analyse what this was (or still is) as it can give you an idea of the foundations of your relationship. Understanding what lies at the base of your attraction to each other can help you to build a strong relationship, especially if problems arise later. You can look back and say 'things are difficult at the moment, but at base my relationship is built on X and this will help to see me through …'. This can get you through tough times as you will realise you have made an important emotional investment in staying together.

Think about what made you arrange more dates once you were over the initial meeting period. Was it his ability to listen or make you laugh? Did she accept you just as you were? Were you intrigued by their openness or shared ideas on politics? Many people experience a phase of euphoria at this stage – a feeling of finding someone who fits them like a glove. If this was you, what was it that made you feel he/she fitted you so perfectly? Try drawing a house. Underneath the house, where

the foundations would be, draw some columns. On the house write the things that are important about your relationship. Now, in the columns beneath, write what you think are the foundations of your relationship. You might want to put words like trust, respect, care, love and so on. These are quite general terms, but write anything that seems important to the two of you. You can do this exercise alone, but sharing it with your partner is also helpful as you can both explore what you think your relationship is built on.

This kind of exercise can be surprising and revelatory. Putting into words feelings and thoughts you may never have expressed before can demonstrate the depth of your attachment to each other. It is particularly helpful if you find it difficult to voice what your relationship means to you. Understanding the deeper roots of what binds you together can be a source of strength if you face a family problem. Bereavement, the sickness of a child or relative, money worries and sexual difficulties are all easier to deal with if you know you have a bedrock of shared values and experience to draw on.

How did you deal with any challenges?

Not many relationships move from the early stages to longer-term togetherness with absolutely plain sailing. After a few weeks or months you probably found there were one or two issues you wanted to sort out. For some people this is connected to moving out of the bubble of 'just the two of you' into mixing with friends and relatives. Think back to this time, when you were introducing your new partner to your world, and ask yourself what happened. Did your parents and relatives like him/her? Did she/he mix with your friends easily? Were there any problems with jealousy of ex-partners? How you faced these challenges could give you some clues to your current style of tackling problems.

?

Try the quiz below to see if you used a particular style of coping with relationship problems, and whether this is still useful to you.

1 If your partner disagreed with you, you were most likely to:

    a) Try to forget about the disagreement and avoid the subject again.

    b) Argue your case and expect them to do the same.

    c) Tell them they were wrong and expect them to eventually agree with you.

2 *When you introduced your new partner to your parents you expected them to:*

a) Accept him/her. If they didn't you might have considered ending the relationship.

b) Like him/her, but would have continued the association despite their response.

c) Accept your choice. It would have been none of their business if they liked or disliked your partner.

3 *Your friends' opinion of your boy/girlfriend was important to you:*

a) Yes, and you chose your partner partly because you knew they would fit in with your crowd.

b) Yes and No. You wanted them to get on with him or her, but if they had not liked your choice you might have changed your friends.

c) No. You chose your partner to suit yourself not your friends.

4 *Your first real argument was about (pick one that has a theme closest to the row you had).*

a) Your inability to make a decision.

b) The problems you had when one or other of you would not join in with a scheme either of you thought important.

c) Your girl/boyfriend trying to control you too much.

5 *Your partner's past was important to you:*

a) Only if he/she talked about it.

b) Yes, it was important to know what experiences they had been through in case it affected how he/she behaved with me.

c) No, unless an ex appeared and flirted with him/her.

Mostly **A**s

You tend to avoid problems. If possible you will steer around difficulties and like to keep the peace. Your partner may accuse you of giving in too readily or bowing to others' demands too quickly. This can sometimes seem to your partner as if you like to hide your head in the sand but your relationship is generally peaceful. If you find that this approach has caused problems in the past with your partner telling you that you are boring or lacking in initiative, you could introduce the following:

- Explain your thought process as you come to a decision. Part of the trouble may be that your partner does not grasp why you are behaving as you are.
- Occasionally allow yourself to voice some disagreement. Experiment with subjects that are not likely to cause an upheaval to see how you feel.
- Think of one thing you regard as really important that you would be prepared to take a stand on. This might be politics, human rights or a work concern. Practise in your head the reasons why this is important to you. You may never be called upon to defend your case, but you will realise that you are capable of reasoning through an issue you care about. Use this skill sometimes with your partner and your relationship will feel more alive.

Mostly **B**s

You like to weigh problems up, looking at all sides of an issue. On the whole, this makes you your own person. You are likely to have your own personal opinion on most subjects. This often means that your relationships are exciting because you enjoy discussing issues with your partner. Your partner may also enjoy this approach, but he/she could also sometimes long for you to go along with the crowd a bit more. If you disagree, it is possible this happens because neither of you is willing to shift from your viewpoint. If this ends up with you unable to find harmony, try the following:

- Ask yourself if you are sticking to your viewpoint because it is important or because you want to uphold a principle, regardless of the cost to the relationship.
- If you feel that your relationship used to have more sparkle because of your enjoyment in debating and discussing, maybe you need to revive some stimulating areas of conversation. Try talking through news reports or topics of local interest in order to revive your relationship. Use ideas that you found interesting in the past to boost your relationship.
- Use your memories of the past to compare what happened then to what you do now. Consider if things have changed and what you might want to do differently in your relationship for the future.

Mostly **C**s

You have always been someone who likes to be in control of a situation. Your partnership is partly founded on your view of yourself as someone who is solid and dependable, and your partner probably saw this as a very attractive quality when you first got together. But this way of seeing yourself and the world may also mean that, beneath the surface, you are somewhat insecure and vulnerable to jealousy. As your relationship has progressed it is likely that your partner has told you that he/she does not like being controlled, but you have found this hard to deal with. To overcome these issues, try the following:

- Ask yourself why you need to control the relationship in the way you do. Have you always been worried that your partner would find someone more attractive or interesting? Do you fear unexpected events that will require you to be open or spontaneous?

Try letting your partner explore some new ways of doing things so you can assess if your usual way of doing things is still useful to both of you.

- Talk to your partner about your need to order events in the relationship. Ask them if they feel, or have felt, constrained by your behaviour and how this has affected them. You may find it a bit of a bumpy ride if they say they *have* felt caged by the relationship, but be patient and calm and you could find a new, and more open, way of relating to one another.

- If you have found yourself in control, it is possible that this is because your partner has needed this approach. They may have chosen you specifically because you seem solid and secure, always knowing what to do. In this kind of relationship, things can run smoothly until you hit a crisis. For instance, if you are ill or have work problems, your partner may feel threatened by your inability to control the situation. Neither of you may want to change the roots of your relationship, but you need to talk about how you would handle a crisis. Pick a subject – finance is a good one to start with – and talk about how you would handle problems in this area. You may never want to alter the way you do things at the moment, but contingency planning can alleviate a great deal of stress if you encounter problems.

Talking about the past

It is not always easy to talk about the past. Most couples are so busy that it is hard enough to find time to talk about what is happening today, let alone what happened six months or six years ago. But if you can find time to do this it will strengthen your relationship and help you to talk about what you want from your relationship – now and in the future.

Here are some ideas to get you started on keeping your memories alive.

✔ **Put an evening, or a rainy Sunday, aside and get out all your old photographs**. If possible, spread them out chronologically and remind yourself of how you met and places you went to. As you look at them, talk about your feelings at the time and the people with you in the pictures. Seize the opportunity to tell your partner what they meant to you at the time. If some of the pictures represent difficult times, talk about these feelings as you share the experience. The idea is to help you both see how far you have come and what you have gained from being together. If you are married, talk about how you felt on your wedding day. If you are living together but not married, find photos of your early days together (perhaps in your first shared home) and discuss how much that time meant to you. Talk about what was special and how the things you did laid the foundations for the future. Avoid concentrating on things that were not so good, although you may need to mention these. Instead, discuss the way you established what was important to the two of you. Home videos are also good for this kind of remembering. The moving image can be very powerful so be prepared for some strong feelings to emerge and support each other if anything proves more emotional than you expected.

✔ **Think back to anything you used to do together that you really enjoyed**. Maybe you went to the dog races, enjoyed concerts or dancing. If there are things that are really beyond you now, think creatively about how you might weave elements of them into your life together. OK, you may not be up to hiking round Thailand again (especially if you have a young family) but you could enjoy long walks in the UK, even a hiking holiday. Sport and leisure can often be tailored to your abilities now. Consider swimming, badminton or yoga for fun and relaxation rather than for competition. Most people have passions they loved but abandon them once they are in a long-term relationship. These pleasures will have helped to form who you are. Reviving them will give you plenty to talk about with your partner. Reading, painting, music of all kinds, DIY – anything that once gripped you – will add to your relationship. Just be careful that a solitary occupation does not mean you ignore your partner. Solitary fishing, complicated needlework, intensive aerobics, fanatically following football and restoring old cars have the potential to detract rather than add to a partnership unless you make a special effort to share the interest.

✔ **Pick a special day and talk about what happened**. Choose a special day that you both remember. It might be a wedding anniversary but could just as well be the day you signed for your house deal, a birthday party or the day you took off for a brilliant holiday. Any important day will do as long as it involved the two of you. Try not to choose a day that was based on another person's celebration – a friend's birthday, for instance – because this will blur the focus on the memories you share. The exception to this is the birth of your children as this is such an important joint event. Now talk about the day from start to finish. Go through the events carefully, making sure you each have a chance to tell your side of the story. Explain why the day was so important and why it has stayed in your memory. A variation on this is for each person to pick a day and tell the other why it is important to them. Use lots of details, conjuring up the feelings of the day. This will help you to feel that your relationship was, and still is, important to you.

✔ **Give a small gift that reminds you of the past**. Giving a small reminder of the past can be fun and tells your partner that you value the time you have spent together. A picture of a place you stayed, something that reminds you of a joke you shared or a bottle of the favourite perfume or aftershave he or she wore at that time. There is no need to make a grand gesture. In fact, something small and inexpensive but that is of importance to the two of you will mean more, and say a great deal, about your care for one another.

✓ **Talk about the past in everyday life**. Mention your memories as regularly as you can. Say 'this reminds me of when we . . .,' or 'do you remember . . . ?'. Use things that made you laugh, times when you felt at your closest and make links between the life you have now and the life you shared in the past. Casually dropping memories into conversation in this way allows you both to acknowledge the bond you share. You might also recall things that were not so happy. If this happens, emphasise how your partner supported you at the time.

Handling difficult memories

Most couples have some memories that they find difficult to talk about. A terrible argument, a child's serious illness, bereavement or a traumatic job loss, for example. It's tempting to want to push these images out of the picture of your relationship. But they formed you as a couple as much as the better times you shared. Without these events your relationship would be a jigsaw with half the pieces missing. You may not want to talk about these things every day, but some discussion about the effect on you both might help you to acknowledge the reality of what happened.

Here are some suggestions to help you discuss difficult memories:

- Pick the right moment. Avoid raising a difficult memory with friends and never use it as a joke with them. For example, telling the story of how your partner lost their job as a humorous story is inappropriate and hurtful. If you do this (and it's surprising how many people do), it may be because you have not fully come to terms with what happened. You need to talk about it in private and in a serious way.

- Use all the communication skills from Chapter One – listen carefully to one another, giving plenty of time for the feelings to emerge.

- Offer affection. For example, if your partner is upset because it is the anniversary of a friend's death, give them a hug and say 'I can see how sad you are that you lost your friend'. Simple warmth will help you both to cope better with unhappy memories.

- Think about times when difficult memories might come to the surface. Anniversaries, birthdays, Christmas and meetings with people connected to the memories can spark reflection on unhappy times. It is helpful if you are aware of dates or events that you know have the potential to cause sadness or anxiety. For example, if your partner has suffered a bereavement, make a note of the date so you can be aware of how he or she might be feeling throughout the year.

- If you have had difficult times together in the past – a big row or temporary separation, for instance – it is useful to acknowledge what happened. If you have recovered but still feel sensitive about it, talking in depth about the memory takes tact and careful handling. Just ask occasionally how your partner feels about the past. Then you can gauge how they are coping with what happened. It will also help you both to be honest about how your partnership is constructed, aiding a feeling of security.

- If you want to raise a difficult memory, start by saying you know it might be hard to think about it. Say 'I know this might be difficult, but do you remember when . . .?' This helps prepare your partner for what you are asking. If you launch straight into your reflections, he or she may be taken unawares and find it hard to respond. You should also avoid the recriminatory style of talking to your partner. For example, 'You never remember the day we . . .' or 'Why is it you refuse to talk about . . . ?' will wind your partner up and push them into responding in the same style. Soon you will be arguing, and definitely not receiving the support you want.

Create new memories

It probably sounds obvious to say that memories need events to allow them to exist at all. If you want good memories of the two of you, you need to do things that will give you pleasure in thinking and talking about them in the future. Here is how to make sure you have happy remembrances:

- Celebrate birthdays, wedding anniversaries or the day you moved in together, the day you first kissed or met. Make your special days personal to the two of you to create a feeling that your relationship is unique and important.

- Take photos or videos of special events. The quality is not particularly important (although lots of people with heads out of frame may not help you to remember who was with you at your birthday party!) Just use them to prompt your memories. If they make you laugh, or feel glad you enjoyed the day, this is an added benefit.

- Develop an enjoyable social life. If you feel worn down by work and domestic tasks, get out more. Take days out for picnics, walks or visiting friends. If you can afford it go out for a meal occasionally. Put as much effort into spending fun time together as you do in organising work and family life.

- Try telling each other 'That's one to remember' or 'I won't forget that' after something special has happened. This will help you both to register what was important. Share why you feel this way.

- If you like writing, keep a journal. Not everything you record will be earth-shatteringly important, but it will help you to look back and recall your relationship at a particular time.

- Decide what you both enjoy and do more of it. This does mean arriving at a compromise if one of you likes something more than the other does but if you trade off certain activities ('I'll watch football with you if you will go for walks with me'), you will find your couple life is livelier and more interesting to remember.

Memories are important because you need them to allow you to see the path you have travelled together. How you managed things in the past gives clues about how you might tackle something today, allowing you to learn from your triumphs and disasters. Sharing memories also helps you to see yourselves as a partnership with a history, allowing you to see how much you have shared. Instead of just putting your memories on the shelf to gather dust, use them to keep your relationship alive.

5

MAKE AN EMOTIONAL INVESTMENT IN THE FUTURE

Have you ever stood in a shop or company reception and read their 'mission statement', usually fixed to the wall on a plaque? This short paragraph usually says something like 'we promise to meet the needs of the customer, to deliver goods of quality and to meet the needs of our shareholders'. Even sandwich bars seem to have these statements, telling you that their sandwiches are packed with fresh ingredients. The idea of a 'mission statement' has become so fashionable lately that we regard it as normal for companies to do this. The process of arriving at a 'mission statement', however, is often not simple. They usually involve lots of meetings as different sections of the company say what they want in the statement. Sales may want something very different to Accounts or Administration. The company usually goes through a whole series of drafts before the planned five bullet points arrive on the plaque on the wall.

If you have seen these 'mission statements', have you ever thought about writing one for your relationship? Creating a set of bullet points for you and your partner probably does sound a bit daunting, but you could look at it as making an emotional investment in the future. Imagine your relationship in the future. What dreams and expectations do you have? How will you make these happen? And when? Some of your hopes for the future might be practical – a new car or house – while others could be more feeling based – to be closer or more secure.

Others might be a combination of the two – to be parents or start a business together. However you describe your investment, what would your personal 'mission statement' look like?

Your Couple Vision for the future

Instead of 'mission statement' (and its business connotations) try thinking of your own 'Couple Vision'. When you first got together could you have described a vision for the future beyond being together? Probably not. Your vision for the two of you has formed over time, but you are unlikely to have put this into words. Instead, it has probably grown as you have both grown together, perhaps rarely voiced. What is sure is that you almost certainly do have a vision of what you think your relationship is, or should be, in your heart. But have you actively decided what a shared vision might look like? Perhaps you are pursuing your own idea of what lies ahead in the hope that your partner is following along behind you?

!

Try the following shared task. Find a pad and pencil and try writing your own descriptions of what you think your relationship aims to do for the two of you. Here is an example to get you started.

We, Darren Smith and Tracy Jones, promise to care for one another. We also agree to live together and to pay jointly for our bills. Once a week Darren will play football and Tracy will visit her sister.

We aim for our relationship to last as long as we want it to and to do everything we can to stay together. We want to have children one day, and will support each other financially and emotionally until, during and after this event.

We want to have a holiday in Florida and the Caribbean in the next five years. We will consider marriage, but do not consider we have to marry in order to have a successful relationship.

As you can see from this example, a vision statement can be quite mixed. In Tracy and Darren's Couple Vision there are parts that deal with emotional issues – caring and support, parts that concentrate on specific plans – holidays and playing football – and areas that discuss less certain plans for the future – having children and getting married. The statement also outlines some key ideas that Tracy and Darren share. They do not believe that marriage is necessary for a happy relationship. They think that financial support is as important as emotional support, putting them in the same sentence as each other. There is an overall sense that this couple is exploring a fairly new relationship (perhaps of a year or two) rather than a couple that has been together for several years. It is interesting to speculate what their vision might look like in two or ten years' time; and how the addition of children might change their outlook.

Here are some ideas to help you as you write your own Couple Vision statement:

How do you want to express your emotions?

What words do you want to use to show your feelings towards one another? Consider: support, care, trust, faithfulness, honesty, openness, passion, thoughtfulness, kindness, equality, challenging or straightforward. As well as using any of these words, choose your own words to suit the character of your relationship. Allow yourself to play with the words you think best fit how you describe your partnership.

What issues are important to include?

Think about things like work and leisure interests. For example, do you want to add in anything about one supporting the other in their work? Or agreeing that one partner can carry on following a particular sport for the next five years? You might include children in this category – either plans to have them or how you want to integrate your couple relationship around any existing children.

What are your core beliefs?

The beliefs you follow might emerge as you write the vision statement, but you could also have some important cultural or religious beliefs you want to include. Think about whether faithfulness is important. (You may think this is a given, but some couples operate relationships where they have other partners but regard their committed partner as their most important relationship.) Do you believe in sharing household tasks or think that just one person should do them while the other works in paid employment? Is your view of a couple just that, the two of you, or would you automatically include the prospect of having children?

It is important to allow equal viewpoints in creating your vision statement. You can tackle this by either writing your ideas separately, followed by work on putting two into one, or by working on your vision together. Either approach is OK, but beware of writing something that ends up as a novel! The idea is to write something that is short (less than 500 words) and is a sketch of your shared vision. You may have to leave some things out, but this is OK if you use the experience of choosing what goes in and what stays out to talk about your relationship.

If you have done this exercise you may have been surprised at the feelings it brings to the surface. Do not worry. Most couples never do this kind of thing and would find talking or writing about their relationship a real challenge. You have been brave to attempt it. So what have you learnt?

● What words did you choose and why?

Take a look at the words you used. Why did you select those particular words and what do they mean to the two of you? Talk about the words and why they are important to you, individually and as a couple.

● What feelings were raised during the construction of your vision statement?

Did you find the exercise easy or hard? Did you have to argue your case strongly to have your viewpoint included, or did you find you agreed on most issues? If you found it hard to agree on what should be included it could be an indicator of a shift in your relationship. If you have encountered a 'life-stage event' (moving in together, having a baby, gaining or losing a job, etc.), your vision of the future is likely to need altering. In this situation it is common for one partner to hang on to previous ideas about the relationship, while the other has moved on to perceiving the relationship very differently. It is this difference in outlook that causes the problem you may have encountered. Working on a vision statement together will help you to re-focus and understand where you are both coming from for your future life together.

● What surprised you?

With a bit of luck you will have encountered a surprise or two as you created the vision statement. Surprise shows you still have life in your relationship, and that you do not know each other inside out. It probably also demonstrates that you are willing to explore change. This indicates the possibility of development in your partnership – a good sign. Tell your partner that you were surprised. For example, if they chose work issues as important when you thought this was the last thing they were concerned about, let them know this is a side of them that is new to you. This kind of learning about your partner should go on throughout your life together. After all, if they were the same person at fifty as they were at twenty-five you might be a bit worried. This is not frightening if you see learning about, and rediscovering, your partner as part of the package in your relationship. They should also be willing to explore you as a person throughout the partnership.

Some variations on creating a shared vision statement

Here are some fun alternatives to writing a vision statement. These could stand alone as shared exercises, or be extra to your vision statement.

Create a couple motto

If you had a motto, what would it be? Think about whether you are pessimists or optimists, serious or fun loving, extrovert or introvert. How do you tackle practical issues? Do you like to prepare or dive into tasks? How about 'If a thing is worth doing it's worth muddling through somehow', 'We never give up', 'Love keeps us together' or 'We get there in the end'.

Make a couple coat of arms

All the best families have a heraldic shield! You may not be a Lord or a Lady, but that need not stop you from having your own shield. Draw a shield or box shape. Divide your shield into four sections. In each section draw something that represents your relationship. For example, if you both love football and salsa dancing, draw a football or a dancing shoe. You might also choose an animal to represent the two of you (like the English heraldic lion and unicorn or Welsh dragon). If you were an animal, what would it be? A giraffe (able to take advantage of the world around you because you are farsighted), a dormouse (may seem a bit boring to others but you are content and cosy with each other), a hedgehog (you can be prickly but underneath still love and care for each other). When you pick your animal, talk through why you have selected the creature and what it says about you. Your interpretation is unique to the two of you so choose anything that you feel comfortable with. If you prefer, you could have two animals facing each other to represent the

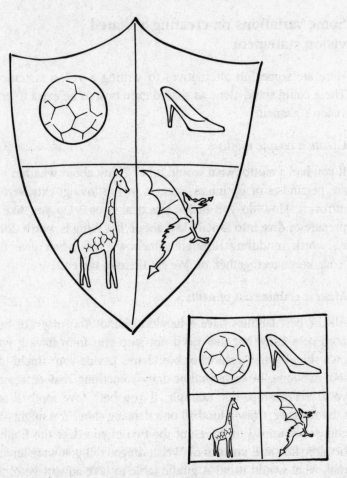

two of you. If you do this, explain why you have represented yourself in the way you have. Do not worry about your drawing skills. A stick figure will do!

Answer the following questions

Read the questions together and answer as quickly as you can. You will probably call out different things so write down your answers.

If we were a:
    Car
    Song
    Flower
    Tree
    Biscuit
    Fruit
    House
    Motorbike
    Computer
    TV Programme

We would be: Name your type, style, species, flavour, etc.

Choose different kinds of the above categories. For example, if you were a biscuit would you be a soft, melting shortbread or a hard, nutty ginger snap? Remember that you are trying to sum up the two of you as a couple rather than as two individuals. Now compare your lists and talk about why you chose the items you did. Work on finding just one description for each item. You may have to incorporate your choices, or even find a new one that fits better.

As you have probably guessed, the true reason for doing these exercises is not to produce a perfect shield, or decide you are both a couple of bananas, but to get you talking about how you see each other and what your emotional investment is in each other. This is not easy. Lots of couples avoid talking in this open way, but it can pay dividends if you allow yourself to try it. You will gradually develop a sense of yourself as a couple, and how you want things to be in the future.

Now you can use what you have learnt to help you think about whether how you see yourselves is what you want. Making an emotional investment for the future means not only deciding what you want later but how you respond to what is happening now. Your coat of arms, motto or list of types (see above) can tell you what you are today, but how might things change in the future?

Looking forward

Lots of couples find looking forward quite difficult because life is unpredictable. Nobody knows what the future may bring – job changes or illness, the birth of children or the death of parents. But positive or negative, change is the one thing you cannot avoid in a long-term relationship. It is important to understand that although your relationship may seem great at the moment, this is not set in stone for the future. As a couple, you will be forced to tackle the issues that change will bring with it. If you think your partnership can only survive in the environment you are in at the moment, your relationship probably has very shallow roots. It is not uncommon for couples to founder if they move from being well off to having less money or, surprisingly, vice versa. (Think of lottery winners who have struggled to stay with their partner after a win.) But you could learn a lot from gazing into a couple crystal ball and making a few predictions for yourself. You may not be able to decide exactly what the future holds, but you could rehearse what you would do in the situations you might find yourself in.

Rehearsing the future

If you have ever been involved in a play (at school, for instance), you will know that rehearsals involve a lot more than just standing on the stage and saying lines. You can also see this if you watch 'the making of …' programmes on TV. The best films take the co-operation of hundreds of people from a multitude of different specialities (actors, make-up, special effects, financial backers, camera men and women, stunt men and women and so on) to produce the image we finally see on film. This is also true of your relationship. Both of you will bring not only many different roles to your relationship but also the script and direction. You are not only actors but playwrights as well. So how would you like the script of your relationship to look? And how might rehearsing the future help the two of you? You could, after all, argue that life does not pan out like a neat script. While this is true, getting close to what might happen, and devising strategies for how you would cope, can help you invest in the future together. One of the key reasons for watching films, but often unspoken, is to observe how the characters portrayed on the screen respond to events, and then to ask yourself if you would behave in the same way. We learn from testing out our own feelings and behaviours against others, including those on film or TV. You can utilise this skill to help you think how you will handle the future of your relationship.

By asking yourself and each other questions about how you would handle different scenarios you can decide if your shared or personal approach is appropriate. Below you will find a number of different couple scenarios. Imagine you are the couple being described and then ask yourself what you would do. Try out the scenarios even if the ages are different from yours – you may be this age yourself soon, or can remember how it felt to be younger. If it helps, adjust the ages to fit yourself today. It does not matter if you feel the scenario is not relevant to you. Allow yourself to play with the ideas you come up with and share them with your partner.

Scenario One

David and Gloria have been together for fifteen years. They both have full-time jobs and decided against children soon after they bought a house together. Now Gloria has found herself unexpectedly pregnant, aged 40. Gloria thinks she wants a termination of the pregnancy. David is not so sure this is the right thing to do (he is 43). What issues do you think are relevant to this decision?

Scenario Two

Mike and Sue (both 30) have money worries. Mike has been a construction worker for many years while Sue works at a local car sales firm. There has been a downturn in the building industry and Mike is struggling to earn a salary. He wants to retrain for another job, but Sue is against this. She feels things will improve soon. What should they do?

Scenario Three

Stella and Andy (26 and 27) have lived together for three years. Stella wants to get married but Andy says they are happy as they are, so why change? Stella is under a bit of pressure from her parents to marry Andy as they are unhappy about her cohabiting. What do Andy and Stella need to take into account in thinking about getting married or not?

Scenario Four

Phil and Jenny (65 and 59) are facing Phil's retirement. Jenny, who is still working part-time, is anxious about how she will cope with Phil at home all the time as she has been used to having the house to herself while he is at work. She does not know how to raise this in case it upsets him. How can they talk about this issue and what do you think needs sorting out?

Scenario Five

Ellen and Gary (38 and 40) have five children. One child is theirs; the other four are from Ellen's former marriage. They are having some problems with Ellen's youngest daughter, a girl of 14. They have recently discovered that she is truanting from school and is often rude and uncooperative at home. What do you think they need to do to sort things out?

As you read these scenarios, ask yourself what you would do in the couple's shoes. Take into account what you think is right and wrong, easy or difficult. What boundaries would you put down and why? Talk about how the issues might be resolved and what steps you imagine yourself taking in this situation. If this seems hard to do, break the issue into 'bite-size pieces'. Think about what the first thing is that should be undertaken. Explain why you feel this. Now say what you would do next. Keep going step by step. As you do this, give your partner time to explain how they would approach the issue.

All the time you are talking about the scenarios you will be learning how your partner:

- Makes decisions – do they like to weigh things up or act quickly on gut instinct?
- Decides what is wrong or right – do they draw their personal morality from a religious background? Or would they tend to act in the way their family has always acted?
- Feels about gender roles. Do they think a man or woman should do certain things or take certain decisions simply because they are male or female?
- Reads and understands situations. Do they like lots of information or just an outline? None of the scenarios are especially detailed. This is to give you both some space to add your own thoughts and speculation to the situation.
- Expects things to be in the future. Do they make judgements about couples based on how things are now or can they make a leap into the future?

You will also learn more about how you both solve issues. As you talk about the scenarios, notice how you both tackle them.

Do you tend to debate the issues or mostly agree what should happen? Are you easily able to imagine how the situation might affect you or do you find it too difficult to imagine yourself in that situation? You could find you fall into some of the following categories:

- An appeaser. You tend to be the one who pours oil on troubled waters rather than get into a disagreement.
- A provoker. You like to stoke the fires of disagreement and often play Devil's advocate even when you do not feel especially involved.
- A listener. You like to hear all the arguments before speaking.
- A speaker. You tend to leap in with your opinion quickly and can summon your arguments quickly.
- A protector. You like to stand up for the lame dog and will tend to act to protect anyone you feel is being unacknowledged.
- An exposer. You like to seek out weakness in others' arguments and point out that they have made a mistake.

The object of this exercise is to help you understand each other as you are now. You may be surprised to learn what your partner feels and thinks, especially if you have been together a while and taken his or her opinions and ideas as the same as they have always been. If you are to make an emotional investment for the future, you also need to know how they come to the conclusions they make. Understanding their favoured approach will give you a chance to discuss whether this is helpful as you think about what you want in the future. Using the categories above, consider whether these are still useful to your relationship:

Appeasers tend to want to smooth over differences and calm discussions down. The positive side of this is that you create an atmosphere where it is easy to talk to each other. The less positive side is that you may find you close conversation and discussion down because of the fear that opinions will get out of hand. It is OK to sometimes express strong ideas to each other and to allow differences to occur. Use your natural diplomacy skills to tease out the ideas you share. This will allow you both to make decisions where action is agreed rather than forced by just one person.

Provokers enjoy the cut and thrust of discussion but may not always want to follow through with their remarks. The positives of provocation are that as you talk about ways out or unusual approaches you can refine what you do think and want. The negatives can mean that as you talk the discussion becomes more and more polarised, with the two of you closer to arguing than examining what you want to do. Use provocation to allow you to see what is really important, and what can be dispensed with. Do not use provocation as a way of avoiding the issues at the heart of the matter. Some people provoke others to create a smokescreen against engaging with the real issues they need to tackle.

Listeners are scarce! Most people find it hard to put aside their feelings and ideas to allow a partner to give full vent to the way they see things. The positives of listening carefully are that you have the benefit of seeing the full picture before you make your remarks. This gives you the chance to weigh up what you think your partner is trying to say before replying. The less positive side is that some listeners are silent not because they are listening and attending but because they are listening and not attending! They may be afraid to say what they feel because they have been shouted down in the past; or mentally practising what they are going to say when they get a chance; or even feeling bored because they think they can predict exactly what their partner is likely to say. Use listening to allow you to hear what your partner is trying to say. Look for what is not said as well as what your partner puts into words. Do they look anxious, confident or worried? Listening attentively is an art. It takes practice, but if you can do this, your investment for the future will reap dividends.

Speakers are often quick thinkers with an ability to speak what they have just thought of. In fact, some people say that it is only in speaking that they realise what they really do think. Use your speaker skills to suggest different approaches and sum up what you think you have agreed. It is common for speakers to be with a partner who is quieter, so use your eloquence with care, ensuring that your partner has a fair chance to say what is on his/her mind. Use 'I feel . . .' at the beginning of statements to avoid speaking for the two of you. This also allows your partner to respond with their feelings and thoughts without having to push your arguments out of the way first.

Protectors identify with those who are going through a bad time and want to take them under their wing. This may not happen only with people, but with ideas and opinions. They may opt for the most unpopular choice, not because they want that outcome but because they feel drawn to defend the position. In a houseful of meat eaters, they will be vegetarian or the only Labour voter in a group of Conservatives. In a discussion they can help to create a balance so that ideas that would otherwise never be considered are aired. But they may also stick doggedly to these ideas in situations where they are not relevant. In any discussion it is important to assess if you are holding on to ideas not because they are useful but because nobody else seems willing to embrace them. Try to use your natural response to help your partner (and yourself) to consider the unusual and different. This will add richness to your partnership.

Exposers are quick to analyse discussion points and usually good at pointing out weak areas. This can be helpful, but also extremely intimidating to a less confident partner. The ability to see quickly the positives and negatives in a discussion is a useful skill but needs to be applied with care. Use this ability to add to your relationship rather than detract from it. For example, you may be able quickly to summarise the way you see things so that your partner can decide if he/she agrees with you. Cultivate listening to what your partner says in reply and pay attention to his/her emotional response. This is also important. Exposers often dismiss emotion in arguments as unhelpful. The truth is that without emotion, no decision can be made. Every decision you made today was influenced by emotion. This is because the emotion and reasoning centres in the brain are linked and influence each other as you think about any decision you make. You may not always be aware of this, but it happens in all decisions – simple and complicated.

———————————————————— **!** —

Now you have some idea of how you talk to one another, try the following questions. It can help to write your ideas and thoughts down or even draw them. Once you have made your lists, select one or two that you could begin working towards now. Discuss the actions you need to take to achieve your plan. Even if the ideas are wacky, they can provide food for thought about the future.

Where do you see yourself in five years?

It helps to divide this question up. Talk about work, where you might want to live, whether you want children or not. You could also add in holiday plans, leisure activities and other interests. Use the opportunity to dream a little. Add in things you may have seen as unobtainable. OK, you may know you will never own a castle in

Scotland, but you could indulge your fantasy by having a Highland holiday!

What is really important to you?

Ask yourself what counts in your life. Is it financial security? Pursuing your career? Buying a house? Raising a family? It is easy in day-to-day life to concentrate on the mundane issues of paying bills and working. Now is your chance to explain to one another what your core concerns are. You may find that your most important life concern is keeping your relationship alive. If you decide this, everything that you decide to do in the future will hang on that decision. For instance, you may want to work long hours to further your career, but coming home earlier allows for you to spend more quality time together, supporting your partnership. Alternatively, you may decide to put a lot of time in at work over a short period in order to buy a house together. Focus on what you think is at the heart of your relationship. This will allow any choices about the next five years to fall into place around this central belief.

How would we cope if something went wrong?

With some idea of what you know is important, talk about what you would do if a problem arose. For example, would your ideas be compromised if you lost your job or became sick? How could you plan to cover these issues? Some problems are not something you can plan ahead for, but if you think through test scenarios on what might be difficult, it will help you if the real thing happens. Even if the actual event is different, the fact that you have had a conversation about how you would handle a similar difficulty will help you. This is rather like practising on a tightrope with a safety net. You can talk about how you would handle a problem, knowing that the practise could get you through the real thing.

Making an emotional investment in the future is good for your relationship. It can help to provide a map as you sail into the future, allowing you both to know where you are coming from and what you want in years to come. Lots of couples find this idea difficult. They may have a vague hope that 'love will keep us together', but as this chapter illustrates, thinking and talking about how you see yourselves and what you want from the future can provide a firm foundation from which to grow and flourish.

6

PUT YOUR COUPLE RELATIONSHIP FIRST

It is easy when you have days full of work and childcare to put your personal relationship at the bottom of your 'to do' list. Sorting the washing, helping a child with homework or checking your e-mails can all seem much more important than time with your partner. But if you do not put your partner first, you run the risk of taking your relationship for granted. Regular time for just the two of you is crucial. Without this precious commodity you will feel out of touch with your partner, eventually losing sight of what you both want and need. Everything you have in your relationship hangs on your togetherness. This may seem obvious – if the relationship is wrong, then nothing else can go right. But lots of couples ignore this, choosing to put most of their attention into work, children or personal interests. When things go wrong, they try to fix the situation without facing the key issue of how they can put their relationship first again.

Do we put our relationship first?

You may wonder if you spend enough time together as a couple. Here is a quiz to help you work out if you share quality time together, and what to do if you think you do not.

1 During the average week we spend:
   a) Less than three hours together alone (not counting sleeping together!)
   b) Between three and five hours together alone
   c) More than five hours together alone

2 We have time to discuss private matters together:
   a) Less than I/we would like
   b) About the right amount of time
   c) Plenty of time

3 We go out together alone:
   a) Less than once a month
   b) Once or twice a month
   c) More than twice a month

4 We go out as a couple with friends:
   a) About three times a month
   b) About twice a month
   c) About once a month

5 We visit relatives or they visit us:
   a) Most weeks
   b) About once a month
   c) Once or twice a month

6 We find it hard to make time for love making:
   a) Frequently
   b) Sometimes
   c) We usually find enough time for love making

7 We argue about our lack of time together:

a) More than once or twice a month

b) Occasionally

c) Hardly ever

8 The last time you went out on a date for just the two of you was:

a) Too long ago to remember

b) Last month

c) Last week

9 The last time you had a quiet evening at home together was:

a) Months ago

b) A couple of weeks ago

c) Last night

10 You would like more time for just the two of you:

a) Yes, we desperately need to see more of each other

b) Sometimes, but we do have regular time for each other

c) No, we have the right amount for us

Mostly **A**s

You are in desperate need of time for just the two of you. You may feel as if you are stuck in a rut of work and sleep with little time to notice each other at all. This may be happening because you are in a particularly busy phase at work or caring for a young family. This kind of distance between you can work for a short time (a few weeks) but eventually you may find yourself wondering why you are in a relationship at all if you hardly see one another. Do not be fooled into thinking that you share time together when you are also with family or friends and that this is the same as time alone together. Time spent with others is not the same as having private time together to cultivate your affection and care for one another.

Improve your pattern

It is time to get out your diaries! Sit down and look for gaps in your week when you could find small amounts of time together. Don't panic if you can only slot in 30 to 60 minutes at first. Start by creating 10 or 15 minutes together during the day or evening. Do something simple – a cup of shared tea or coffee is a start – and allow yourself to relax together. Once you get into this habit, it is then easier to find longer periods of time together. Once a month, book a date you can both enjoy. A meal in an inexpensive restaurant (or a take-away at home if finances are stretched), a trip to the cinema, a quiet drink at a country pub, a walk in the park or an evening at home with a favourite video are all good for improving your sense of yourselves as a couple rather than as two members of a business or a childcare company!

Mostly **B**s

You are working towards enjoying time as a couple. You have a good balance of time together and realise how important it is to make time alone. This is probably because you have worked hard to find time to set aside for just the two of you. It is possible that you have been through times when you were aware that you had little time together and took steps to make sure this did not happen again. Or perhaps you are in a phase of life that means you are more often alone as a couple than in previous years – the parents of older children, for instance. If you experience a see-saw in finding time alone together (some months are OK, others less good when you see each other rarely), you should plan ahead in order to have the time you need.

Improve your pattern

Look back at any periods when you were less likely to spend time together. Analyse why this happened. Was it unavoidable because of work commitments, or did it seem to happen because your time together slipped out of your mind? It is useful to do this because if you recognise a pattern in your behaviour, you can work to improve the quality of your time together, if not always the quantity, during busy times. Make sure you sit down and concentrate on one another rather than grabbing a few minutes over breakfast or at bedtime. It can help to have a focus to encourage you to put time aside. Try playing cards, chess, backgammon or any other game, do a crossword together or read different parts of your favourite newspaper so you can share and discuss what you find. Some couples enjoy playing sport together – tennis, badminton and so on – but be careful that this does not become over-competitive or involve lots of other people. The object of your shared time is to have some fun and invest in the bond between you, not have you fighting over whether a point is in or out!

Mostly **C**s

You spend lots of time together and have found a way to make this work. It is possible that you have a shared business you run together, or have grown-up children, so you can choose when to see each other more or less when you want. If you spend this amount of time together, you have probably worked out what you enjoy doing together and what you dislike. It is important to think about what you need for your time together and to vary how you fill your time.

Improve your pattern

Spending lots of time together is good for your relationship, but you need to consider what you do and whether it is good for both of you. If you regularly find yourself doing things that only your part-ner enjoys, rather than having both your needs met, talk about how you could achieve a better balance. You could also slip into the dangerous area of taking your partner for granted, believing that the pattern of being together you have created is still satisfying. Try making a list of all the things you do and then adding anything you would like to try. For example, if you go to the pub a lot, why not try a completely different venue for a drink. Or consider play-ing a game you may not have tried. Variety is the spice of life! Experiment with different ideas to help you enjoy the time you have together, thereby improving your sense of closeness as you discover what you want. If you spend a lot of time together on shared ventures – perhaps running a shop together or both of you working from home – it is important to consider whether you have quality time together or just take one another for granted. You should also think about whether you have your own identity or always feel like a member of a couple. If you never have time for yourself, cultivate some time that allows you to feed the relation-ship with new ideas and activities. Following your local football team, attending arts events in the area or learning to line dance, for example, could all add interest to your relationship and increase your self-esteem. Stimulating your conversation within the partnership will help your relationship to feel lively and interesting – and keep it a going concern.

Distractions – how not to put your relationship first!

When I work with couples in counselling I often ask them about time spent together. The majority tell me that they rarely have time to be alone together, let alone talk, make love or have fun. But this is rarely the whole story. As they tell me about their week, it is clear that there is often time to be together but that they allow distractions to prevent them from being alone. Sometimes this is due to the problems they have encountered in the past. For example, they may fear that if they have time on their hands they will argue, so they seek distractions to avoid being trapped together. More often it is due to being out of practice in thinking of themselves as 'just a couple'. So here are some well-known distractions and how to overcome them:

TV

Are you an avid soap watcher or sci-fi fan? Do you switch the TV on the minute you set foot in the house? Some people treat TV as a murmur in the background and talk happily while it is on. But most people find themselves drawn to the image on the screen and conversation soon dries up. Or they sit up late at night, long after their partner has gone to bed, watching the end of a film or programme.

The only solution to this problem is to make liberal use of the off switch! If it sounds too much like 'cold turkey' to turn the TV off all evening, try watching only one or two selected programmes in an evening. Use the rest of the time to chat, cook and enjoy a meal together (not in front of the telly!) or listen to music. If the kids want to watch TV, try having a room where you can escape the box for a while – perhaps a bedroom or dining room. You should also consider if you are using the TV to avoid being together or because you find it difficult to discover things in common. Now is the time to turn off and reconnect before you forget why you chose to be together.

Children

You may not see your children as distractions, but they can sometimes prevent you from focusing on yourself as a couple. There is a balance to be struck between racing your son or

daughter to sports, dance, drama, scouts, guides or music class-
es every evening and having time for the two of you. After a long
day at work, the worst thing you can do is spend the evenings
taxiing your progeny round every class going and then waiting
to collect them outside a community hall on a cold evening in
December.

Place some limits on what your children can do. Some class-
es are OK, but five nights a week are too many. Not only do you
need to relax and see your partner, but the children also need
'down' time to just be at home with their brothers and sisters
(if they have them). They probably also need an early night!
Explain that they can have some interests, but they need to
choose from a selection rather than pursuing every hobby that
comes their way. The same goes for homework and reading
practice. If you spend hours poring over your child's homework
books with them, pushing them to be the best in the class,
you will soon be more in touch with your child's view on life
rather than your partner's. Let them find their own level.
Encourage rather than cajole. If they seem to need hours of help
with their work, talk to their teacher as they may be struggling
with the level of work. It is not your role to do their homework
for them.

If you recognise yourself in the parenting roles above, then
you may be living through your children instead of living
your own life. If you want them to go to every group activity
under the sun, maybe *you* crave some fun. If you are pushing
them to do well at school, maybe it is *you* that is seeking
intellectual stimulation, not them. If this rings a bell, start
putting yourself and your partner first instead of the children.
This may sound a bit tough. It is true that your children do need
your one-to- one love and attention as they grow and develop.
But you need to find a balance that allows you to be partners
as well as parents.

Remember, without your solid partnership your child's ability to enjoy clubs and do well at school will shrivel. Think of your relationship like a coat hanger with the children hanging off you, the main bar of the coat hanger. If the hanger gets too weighted towards the children, it will collapse. Maintaining a successful balance allows you to sustain your loving partnership and keep your children safe and strong.

Friends and relations

It is important to spend time with your friends and relations. A wide circle of friends is stimulating and enjoyable, while supportive relatives can help you survive the ups and downs of daily life. But if you spend several evenings a week with your friends, or pop in on your mum every day, your partner may wonder exactly how important they are to you. If you also spend lots of time socialising with a group of friends as a couple you might feel as if you have had quality time together when you really spent the whole evening at the other end of a dining table or pub bar from your partner. It is important to vary how much time you spend on your friendships and your time alone together. If you spend several evenings with friends or relatives, agree to give your partnership equal attention. Book time out in your diary so that you know you have a 'partner exclusive' evening coming up. You may want to get out, or simply curl up on the sofa. Either way, chilling out together gives plenty of opportunity for casual conversation or more serious discussions about your life together.

If, as you read this, you find yourself thinking 'how would I cope without seeing my best mate/favourite sister/great brother-in-law most days?' you may be running away from something in your relationship. Perhaps you are hanging on to an allegiance to friendship or family because you fear giving yourself completely up to your partner. Or maybe your emotional investment has always been with friends rather than a one-to-one relationship. If this sounds like you, you must consider what you really want – an intimate partnership or a wider circle of friends. Some people are scared of close relationships because they worry that they may fail their partner in some way. They often keep up with a wide range of friends and family, enjoying a light-hearted set of connections that never call for deeper or more serious considerations because they are not really sure how to do this. This can be related to childhood experiences – parental divorce or conflict can lead to an avoidance of close relationships in adulthood because of the fear of hurt the child may have absorbed as it grew up. It may also be the result of a broken relationship in your past, leading to a feeling that it is safer to stay within a group than risk more heartbreak in an exclusive twosome.

Talk to your partner of your concerns about how much you see of a particular friend or relation. Do not try to cut off your friend overnight. Instead, gradually cut down your contact until it is more in balance with your relationship with your partner. You do not need to lose the friendship, just adjust your time together so that your relationship also receives the kind of attention your friend does.

A complication of 'family as distraction' is an unforeseen crisis. Your parents may fall ill or, as they age, need more of your attention. This can be a tough situation to resolve. It is likely that your relationship will feel under pressure as you spend time trying to care for your parents *and* keep your partnership alive. In this situation, do not pressure yourself to give equal time to your partner. Just make sure that you let them know how much they mean to you if you spend time away from home visiting sick relatives. An affectionate hug, thoughtful note on the fridge door or a few minutes sharing a cup of tea will keep your relationship ticking over until you can be together more. It can be extremely helpful to occasionally grab a day or two together away from the situation. This will allow you to relax and feel refreshed before returning to what may be an emotionally draining environment.

Personal interests

Without hobbies and interests life would be very dull. Following a favourite football team, playing tennis, fishing, reading, going to the cinema, cookery (or watching a famous TV cook make meals!), surfing the net, listening to CDs, making music, singing in a choir, to name but a fraction of the things people enjoy, gives a vibrancy to life that makes all the difference between boredom and involvement in life. But these interests can have a down side. As a therapist I often see couples where one partner's interest has taken over their life. They organise all their free time to fit around following a rugby team or favourite pop star around the country. Or spend hours fishing or on DIY while their partner feels left out in the cold.

Most relationships can tolerate some of this kind of behaviour. You may even see it as endearing of your partner to want to be at every away, as well as home, match of the local team, especially if they are way down the league. But if this goes on for months and years, with special family events taking second place to a personal interest, then what seemed endearing when you first got together can become irritating and annoying. The hobby that was interesting to chat about can become a source of disagreement when it goes from a few hours a week to all weekend every week. Some people even describe their partner's adherence to a particular interest as being as bad as an affair because they feel that the love they want to receive is being given to something else. In fact, it is often more painful because the attraction to another person may feel tangible. But it can seem impossible to take on an intangible quantity such as a football team or dance class!

If you recognise yourself as the kind of person who is inclined to spend hours pursuing a hobby then you need to do some thinking about what message this gives your partner. Do they accept your devotion or seem upset that you spend lots of time on it? Do you often put your interest before other events that you would usually do as a couple? Do you know that you use your hobby as a bolthole from the relationship? If you answer 'yes' to at least two of these then you may be using your leisure pursuit to escape from the relationship in some way. Perhaps you feel under pressure or unhappy about some element of the partnership. Whatever the reason, your relationship will not be improved by your prolonged absence, because you are creating a vicious circle that may mean the partnership is never the close and caring relationship you had in mind when you set out. Of course, it is true that some people welcome their partner having something to take them out of the house on a regular basis. If you breathe a sigh of relief when your partner takes up their snooker cue or yoga mat and goes out for the evening, you are certainly not alone! The desire for a little personal space is natural in most relationships. It is when the sigh of relief becomes one of distress that you need to be concerned.

The best way to tackle the issue is to talk to each other about what you think is a reasonable time spent on personal interests. Look at your time together and decide if it is enough for the two of you. Think about what you might do together that interests you, alongside the daily chores. It is possible that the reason your partner, or you, seek so much time apart is that what is on offer at home seems boring and routine by comparison. Build up enjoyable things to do as a couple. Even simple things such as picnics in the park are OK as long as you have some fun together. A word of warning – avoid shopping together! This is not a leisure pursuit and tends to drain rather than build up a relationship. Unless you like pottering for antiques or specialist items as a hobby, shopping can be a punishment rather than a reward, especially clothes shopping when you will probably see more of the changing room curtain than each other.

You should also consider whether you might be able to share a hobby. If it is a spectator sport, could your partner come with you occasionally? If you are fishing all day, could your partner join you for lunch? If you are the partner of someone hooked on a particular hobby, think of ways in which you could sometimes share their interest. For instance, could you look for links on the net for information on a particular team? Accompany them to a game? Or video tape a programme on water features in gardens? If you demonstrate a willingness to be open to their world, you may find that they want to involve you or seek to give it less attention than they have done. Sharing an interest says you care about the person and want the best for them. This has a positive effect on a relationship and may even tempt them to spend less time on an absorbing interest.

If you really feel you cannot share a hobby then try to establish some boundaries on time spent on it. For example, you might decide that one day (or equivalent) a week is about right. Or 'X' hours a week might seem fair. Another approach is to agree that you will spend equal time on the relationship as on the hobby, although this might include socialising with friends as well as time alone together. Again, try not to make this time together task led. If your shared time is spent stripping wallpaper or weeding borders, it is not so surprising that the attraction of playing on the Playstation might seem more alluring.

Developing new ways to be together

If you feel that your time together has been a bit lacklustre of late, use the planner below to help you brainstorm some ways to enjoy being together again:

Answer the questions below. Try to do this as a couple, perhaps when you are sitting quietly without interruption.

The things I like to do most are . . . Choose from –

> Physical & sporty
> Quiet & reflective
> Chatty & sociable
> Musical & lively
> Musical & listening
> Group orientated
> Solo or couple orientated

Some examples of these are . . . Give a list of examples that reflect your favoured choices, such as sports, creative or learning activities.

I could share this activity with you in the following ways . . . Think of ways in which you could create couple activities. For instance, you may go swimming or attend a play together.

Simple things we could enjoy together include . . . Pick from the list any that appeal.

> Walking in the country
> Listening to music at home
> Watching a video together
> Enjoying a meal (or take-away)
> A quiet drink at the pub
> Making love
> Visiting a local site of interest (garden, stately home, castle, museum, etc.)
> Taking part in a sport together

Once you have selected the style of being together and perhaps some activities you might like to follow, think about how you could factor this into your life. Get out your diaries or calendar and work out how you could make any of your choices work for you. When you have chosen your evenings or days make a note and stick to your choice. The most important part of this exercise is to find something that you both feel relatively comfortable with and keep practising being together until you get the most enjoyment from it. If you make a mistake in a choice, do not worry. Try again until you find something that makes you happy.

Where is your heart?

Some people feel that they put their relationship first but in reality have a focus elsewhere. For instance, they may say to their partner 'Yes I do work hard but it is all for you and the kids' or 'You always come first in my affections but I have to have frequent holidays alone to find myself'. They may repeat this even when you protest that you would be happy poorer if you could see them more or ask them to 'find themselves' with you. When this happens it may be because the person is not matching up what they think they are doing with what is really happening. Their focus is not on the partnership (or family) but on work, leisure or something else of importance to them. They may want to believe that they are working hard or travelling because it will benefit you in the long run, but the frustrated partner rarely understands this benefit.

Why does this happen?

There are lots of reasons why you or your partner may focus on something outside of the relationship but tell you that what they are doing is actually *for* the relationship. Here are a few common reasons:

- **It is a smokescreen**. The relationship is in trouble but neither person can admit it. One (or both) justifies working very hard, for example, as their contribution to the relationship.

When arguments happen, they may both feel justified in saying 'I'm doing my best. It is you. You're not trying'.

- **It is a fear of self-expression**. The man who says 'Of course I love you, didn't I work overtime to buy you a dishwasher' or the woman who says 'You should know how I feel, I cook you Jamie Oliver meals every day' are using their focus on something else to express their feelings. The problem is that often the other partner does not understand the message! They may long for their partner to say 'I love you' and will not see the meal or the dishwasher as an expression of this sentiment.

- **The enjoyment of the activity (work, leisure, etc.) obliterates sensitivity to a partner**. This can happen when someone becomes mildly obsessed with what they are doing because they get a lot of reward from doing it. If you love work because you feel really good at it and get lots of praise from colleagues, or find working out at the gym helps you maintain a honed body that others admire, it may be hard to focus on your relationship when you need to. Of course, there is nothing wrong with enjoying work or exercise, but if your partner feels isolated and hurt by your concentration on these kinds of activities, you need to reassess where your heart is. If this sounds like you, maybe you are not getting enough affirmation in your relationship. Ask yourself if you feel valued by your partner. If you are not sure, or even feel put down by them, you could be investing in other things to make up for the lack of positive support. Talk to your partner about how you are feeling.

- **It is the result of a life change**. Life changes can trigger reassessments of personal behaviour. Bereavement, serious illness, work difficulties (such as redundancy or even promotion), family problems (children playing up or becoming ill) can all cause the focus of one, or both partners, to drift away from the relationship. All life changes involve some stress. In an effort to alleviate this stress, people often immerse themselves in a hobby or work. Other common diversions are DIY and building work. It is not uncommon for a couple to take on a major house renovation project to avoid looking at problems in their relationship or in some other area of life. This approach can sometimes work for a short period of time as it provides a focus for thinking and relaxing. But if you begin to feel like ships that pass in the night, instead of docking together at the end of the day, you need to think about what caused you to avoid being alone together. Look for triggers in the recent past (or sometimes the distant past) that have not been discussed or resolved. Then make a plan to sort out problems or talk about whatever has unsettled you.

Use the chart below to assess when you could find time to be together. Look for chunks of time that are 30 minutes or longer. Once you have identified some areas in the week that might be useful to you, look at the list below. See if you can match the activity to the time available.

Suggested activities to share

Share a drink (alcoholic or non-alcoholic)
Share a meal (without distractions, if possible)
Watch a favourite TV programme/DVD/video
Listen to a favourite CD
Go for a walk
Go swimming/play a sport/watch a sport
Make love
Go out for some fun – anything that takes your fancy
Have a day out
Have a weekend away

Our time together table

Monday	Tuesday	Wed'day	Thursday	Friday	Saturday	Sunday
Morning	*Morning*	*Morning*	*Morning*	*Morning*	*Morning*	*Morning*
Afternoon	*Afternoon*	*Afternoon*	*Afternoon*	*Afternoon*	*Afternoon*	*Afternoon*
Evening	*Evening*	*Evening*	*Evening*	*Evening*	*Evening*	*Evening*

As you fill out your chart look for 'touching places' as well as longer periods of time. Half an hour spent sitting in the garden or lingering over a glass of wine together helps to keep your contact alive. A two-week holiday together when you have hardly seen one another for months can be a recipe for disaster as your expectations will be sky high and inevitably destined for disappointment. Regular investment in your relationship will help you both to feel in touch and well able to understand each other's needs without fear and anxiety. Then you really will have put your relationship first.

7

SEXUALLY SPEAKING – QUALITY, NOT QUANTITY, IS WHAT COUNTS

When did you last make love? Ask most couples, especially those with kids and busy working lives, and you probably get an embarrassed silence as they try to work out whether it was last week or last month! The idea that a married or living-together couple has sex at least three times a week is responsible for more sexual unhappiness than almost any other idea that people think they know about sex. The problem is that this preoccupation with how often you make love is the wrong question. The question you should be asking yourself is 'Is the quality of our sex life any good?' You might make love every day, but it could be as exciting as cleaning your teeth. Or you might make love once a year, but it is so mind blowing that you can wait twelve months for the next time!

Some sex facts

Let's start with some facts about sexual relationships. We are all surrounded by so much mythology about sex that it can be hard to untangle the truth. But what is known about sexual behaviour in committed couples can be enormously comforting if you think your own sex life is not the full-on variety you see on TV or read about in magazines.

Real sex lives ebb and flow

The natural pattern of human sexual relationships is for the desire for sexual contact to alter with the stage of life, life events and day-to-day stresses and strains that you experience. Some weeks or months you may feel like lots of sex, sometimes very little. Sexual desire is easily affected by how you are feeling; anger, tiredness and stress all take their toll on desire. The latter two are responsible for most downturns in sex. For example, if you have worked a long day, had a falling out with your manager, and returned home to find a sick child, sex will be the last thing on your mind. Feeling upset with your partner over something fairly minor can also cause you to switch off sexually. Some people find making up after a row can be sexually stimulating, but sex while you are still angry is usually unsuccessful. Resuming sex after childbirth or a family crisis can often leave you both feeling emotionally and physically fragile, so your sexual desire may seem erratic for a long time. Sexual desire is not switched on at puberty to run at full flood into old age! It is more like a tap that can get turned on and off according to your mood and phase of life.

Real sex is affected by how long you have been together and how committed you are

The longer your relationship, the less frequently you make love. This probably sounds like bad news. If you are a man and aged 35–44, in a relationship of 2 to 5 years' length, statistically, on average, you make love 6 times a month. If you are a woman in the same circumstances and of the same age, you also make love 6 times a month. But if you have been together 6 or more years then this figure drops to 5 for men and 4 for women. Older men and women in long-term relationships make love less than this. But the researchers found that the couple feeling more secure together accounted for some of the falling off in sexual frequency[1]. This makes sense. If you are less secure in a new relationship, you may make love more to promote the bonding effect that sex gives relationships. Once your bond is safe, sex becomes less of an issue and less important. Also, this research figure is an average of activity, so some months couples may have had less or more sex. The other, and more important, issue is that couples in long-term relationships state that the quality of their sex life is superior to sex in less-committed relationships, even though the frequency of the sex is more in shorter relationships.

Real sex needs working on

If you want to have a fulfilling sex life that lasts years rather than weeks, you need to think about it and work together on what you want. In the initial stages of falling in love, sex can seem very exciting and passionate. You are likely to pay little attention to what you are doing, following your instincts and immediate desires instead. But this phase fades quickly. Once you have made a commitment to each other and begun to feel like a couple rather than casual partners, your feelings about sex will almost certainly change. You may notice that you are less instinctive, and want to talk about what you do and do not like. You may feel that this is an indicator that the relationship is in trouble – if you have to think about sex surely things are going downhill? The truth is that you are simply in a more mature relationship where working out how you want to run your sexual relationship is par for the course. The good news is that as you develop a sexual style together you will gain from feeling part of a couple that shares a deep bond.

[1] Statistics from *Sexual Behaviour in Britain* by Kaye Wellings, Julia Field, Ann Johnson & Jane Wadsworth (Penguin)

Talking and behaving intimately is good for you and your sense of security.

Working on your sexual relationship also allows you to be adaptable and flexible in your attitudes. This will mean that you have a wide repertoire of sexual activities that you can use at different times. Too tired for sex? Have a gentle massage instead. Got lots of time to enjoy love making? Try lots of different foreplay techniques. Time for sex limited? Use different styles of touching and arousing your partner so that you can enjoy a quick climax. If you stick to the same old thing every time you make love, your routine may not stand up to the changing world you will both share as you grow together. Soon sex may become a casualty of your inflexible attitude. You do not have to hang from the lampshade every night, but you could enjoy a full range of sexual expression together. Sex is a demonstration of your love for one another – try not to limit that expression.

Real sex is fun

Real sex should make *you* happy. Some people seem to have missed this basic fact! They think they should have sex to make their partner happy, because they are expected to or because they think they would be abnormal in some way if they did not. If you spend your life having sex only to please someone else, you have missed the whole point of sex. The same goes for you carrying out sexual activities you are not happy about just because your partner thinks they are a good idea. Real sex should improve your sense of closeness, make you laugh sometimes and be a source of private pleasure. All of these are derived from the quality of sex, not the quantity. Anxiety and fear make good sex impossible. Shared affection, respect and openness make good sex not just possible but guaranteed.

Thinking about your sex life

Thinking about what you do in bed may be a new concept. Some people never think about what they enjoy, or dislike, still less talk about it. They fall into the 'sex should be spontaneous to be enjoyable' school. While it is true you cannot script sex (only Hollywood can do this!), every act of sex has been thought about and planned before it takes place. Don't believe me? Think of all those hours you spent getting ready to meet your lover. Why did you do this? Because sex might have been going to happen. What about those fleeting thoughts about sex while you are working? Or feeling a mild sexual response as the vibration of the bus gets going on the way to work? Or seeing an attractive woman in the street? You may not have seen these as part of planning or thinking about sex – but they are. When you make love the act itself is the cumulative effect of your thinking and feeling sexually during the day. Some of these feelings are unconscious. Desire is prompted by a thousand and one daily experiences, most of which you are not consciously aware of.

Take a look at the list below. You may want to do this, with your partner or alone to share with your partner later. It is your choice. Grade each item out of 10: 10 is a high grade, i.e. arousing and enjoy doing; 1 is a low grade, not arousing and not enjoyable. As you fill out the list, try to be honest. You may want to appear more liberal than you really are, or try to disguise your sexual tastes in case you appear too wanton! Just write down what you feel. It can help to fill out this list quickly so your unconscious can play a role in what you write. Taking a long time to deliberate may mean you want to hide some aspect of your sexuality.

Activity	Mark
Kissing and caressing	
Stroking the whole body, but not breasts and genitals	
Direct stimulation of the genitals and/or breasts and/or prolonged manual genital stimulation for male and female	
Vaginal intercourse with the man on top/woman beneath	
Vaginal intercourse with the woman on top/man beneath	
Oral sex – for both male and female	
Vaginal intercourse in a variety of positions	
Dressing up for sex (silky underwear, etc.)	
Using a vibrator or another kind of sex toy	
Stimulation of the anal area	
Tying up hands or wearing a blindfold	
Using private fantasy to enhance sexual experience	
Using sexually explicit publications to aid arousal	
Talking in sexually explicit terms to one another (sometimes called 'dirty talk')	

This list is by no means exhaustive. You can probably think of some others you would like to include. If you want to do this, just add them to the list and give them a grade. Now look back over your list. Assess why you gave the grade you did. For example, have you tried all the items listed? Did you grade some of the items lower because you thought you would not like them, rather than tried them and disliked them? Did you grade some items high because you know they are sexually arousing for you or because you think they might be? Did any of the items cause you to feel anxious? For example, did you think 'I ought to give this a high grade because I think lots of other people do it but I don't like it/don't think I would enjoy it'? Did you grade any of the items because of the way you think your partner would feel about them rather than how you feel about them?

Reflecting on your list is important. It will help you to begin to think about the quality of your sex life rather than the quantity. What you do together, and how you feel about it, is central to enjoying rewarding love making. If you did this exercise with your partner it might be interesting to see if their grades match yours. Look back at your lists and grades. As you do this, look for the items that are most disparate. For instance, you might find that one of you really enjoys prolonged periods of stimulation while the other does not enjoy this as much. Talk about what is causing this difference.

Talking about sex

If you want to talk about sex with your partner as you fill in this chart you may find it slightly embarrassing. You are not alone with this problem. Lots of couples find it nerve racking to discuss sex. Here are some tips if you fall into this category:

- Avoid having in-depth discussions about sex in bed, especially after (or during!) love making. Try cuddling up on the sofa when you are quiet and unlikely to be interrupted. The reason for this is that if you run into a problem, your discussion will seem less heated and critical than if you are in the place you usually make love. Plus, your bedroom (or usual place you make love) can stay a place of retreat.

- Stay calm and caring. Sex is a very sensitive subject for most people. If you want to talk about sexual technique, or when you choose to make love, for instance, your partner may interpret this as a criticism. Maintaining a 'we can do this together' attitude is better than an 'I'm going to tell you what I think' approach.

- Say what you really like. Be specific rather than woolly. For instance, say 'I really love it when you kiss my neck behind my ear' rather than 'I like it when you kiss me'. Offer praise and words of affection for sex you enjoy.

- If you want to tell your partner you are not happy with something, avoid saying 'I hate it when you . . .'. For example, say something like 'I really like it when you caress my back and I would love it if you also stroked my bottom'. In this way you are helping your partner to feel good about their prowess as a lover rather than making them feel inadequate. If they feel useless as a lover, they will gradually lose confidence and sex will become a battleground.

- Listen carefully to what your partner says. If they feel inhibited in sex, or tell you clearly that they do not want to carry out a sexual activity you would like to experiment with, respect their decision, even if you do not agree with them. Never tell them they are frigid or boring. Work on understanding why your partner feels the way they do.

- Avoid focusing on technique to the exclusion of everything else. You may feel that telling your partner they are too rough or not responsive is what they need to hear. But there may be a reason why they are behaving the way they are. Help them, and you, understand what is happening by talking about the emotions surrounding the action.

How arousal works for men and women

Men and women have different arousal patterns. Women respond to arousal in four stages, while men have three.

The four stages of female arousal

1 As a woman becomes aroused blood suffuses the genital region. She begins to produce lubrication from specialist glands in the vaginal walls. Her vaginal lips and vagina swell and become darker in colour. Inside, her womb and cervix begin to lift up inside the body, pulling the vagina up and lengthening it.

2 The woman becomes more sexually excited by manual stimulation or intercourse. The tip of the clitoris hardens and becomes longer. As stimulation intensifies the clitoris slips back under the hood of skin at the top of the vaginal opening. This is often known as the 'plateau' stage as women can often enjoy lengthy stimulation in this phase.

3 Orgasm occurs and is felt as a series of rhythmic pulses throughout the pelvic area. The number of muscle contractions varies from five to twenty-five. Women are also capable of multiple orgasms and may go on to have several orgasms that usually gradually fade in intensity.

4 With the climax over, blood drains away from the woman's vaginal lips and clitoris. They resume their resting state and the womb and cervix descend to their usual position.

It is worth noting that the vagina is like an upside down wine bottle, with a narrow neck opening out into a wider area. The neck is about two inches long and imbued with lots of nerve endings. This area is called the 'orgasmic platform' by sex therapists, as it is the key area of the vagina that contracts during orgasm. It feels bigger because of the large number of nerve endings it possesses. The upper part of the vagina is more responsive to pressure than direct stimulation. It is for this reason (despite the national obsession with penis size!) that large penises are no better at arousing a woman than an average size. Most of the vagina is not directly stimulated by the penis.[2] In fact, many women say that it is more exciting to be penetrated by a short, thick penis than a long, slim one.

The three stages of male arousal

1 As a man begins to feel aroused blood flows to the genital region. The penis fills with blood and starts to stiffen. Special valves in the veins supplying blood to the penis prevent blood from leaving the penis. He experiences pleasant feelings of warmth and constriction. As rubbing (either by hand or in the vagina) stimulates the penis a small amount of liquid may be released from the opening at the tip of the penis. This liquid sometimes contains sperm. The testicles become tighter, darker in colour and lift closer to the body.

2 The man experiences rhythmical contractions of the muscles in the pelvic region, causing ejaculation and orgasm. The liquid ejaculated from the penis contains the sperm. The sensation of orgasm is slightly ahead of ejaculation, although most men do not notice this difference.

3 The penis gradually returns to its usual flaccid state as blood leaves the penis and pelvic area. The testicles return to their usual position.

The most sensitive part of the penis is the glans, also called the head. If stimulation is applied to the area on the underside of the head, either by licking or gentle rubbing, the man usually experiences intense feelings of arousal. The average erect penis size is

[2] From *The New Hite Report* by Shere Hite (Hamlyn)

5 to 6 inches. The size of the flaccid (soft) penis is no indicator of erect size. In fact, most penises are similar in size when erect.

Female arousal usually takes longer than male arousal. Men are able to reach orgasm and ejaculation in a few minutes (especially when young) whereas many women take at least fifteen minutes to reach orgasm, and usually longer than this. This variation in time is explained by the woman's 'plateau' stage of arousal. She needs longer to reach orgasm and so most heterosexual love making is a matter of balancing this difference in arousal times. This simple biological difference in how men and women respond to arousal is little known and the cause of a great deal of tension in love making. Many men think that a woman should respond as quickly as a man should while women tend to blame themselves for not being fast enough in their response to sexual stimulation.

Creating a balance

If reproduction was an act undertaken by people alone, sex would probably not seem as complex an issue as it can be! But, with or without the intention to have a child, sex is a couple act and so needs the attention and care of both partners if it is to be successful.

Are you in the right mood?

Many couples imagine that they can make love no matter what is happening in their lives. It is as if they see sex as something that should be excised from the rest of life and be unaffected by anything else that is happening to them. Sex is an appetite and like any appetite can be affected by what is happening to you in other areas of life. Think of another appetite – eating – as a comparison. You know that your appetite varies according to what you are doing. Some days you may want a light meal, on others you could eat a horse. Tiredness can kill appetite so that you may want a quick snack rather than be bothered to prepare a three-course meal. What you enjoy eating also varies from day to day. You may have fads on certain foods, only to grow bored with them and avoid eating them for weeks. Now compare sex to eating. Many couples try to have sex when they are too tired, avoid experimenting with different sexual activities or try to persuade their partner to have a long sex session when they only want a quickie. This is the equivalent of making your lover sit at a dinner table to eat roast beef with all the trimmings when they only want beans on toast! Or eating the same meal every day for years. Long before you even get to the first kiss, how you feel about love making will affect the outcome.

Next time you think you want to make love, or your partner asks you, here are some questions to ask yourself.

- Am I tired or under stress? How might this affect my response to sex?
- Have we had a disagreement or are we suffering a communication breakdown? Would sex help or hinder this?
- What style of sex would I like? Fast and passionate, slow and sexy or tender and gentle?
- How is my partner feeling? Am I suggesting sex when they want it as well or asking at an inappropriate time?

Enjoy the journey

Are you a rugby player in love making? I am not suggesting you dress up in shorts, shirt and boots to have sex! No, I am asking if your sex life is the emotional equivalent of scoring a try – a fast charge up the pitch followed by a slam over the line at the end. Lots of couples say this is the pattern of their love making. Fast sex is not always bad. It can be exciting and thrilling. But if you make love in this way every time, it can lock out the sensual pleasures of relaxed love making and prevent a feeling of satisfaction, even if you both have an orgasm. (Fast sex also often prevents a woman from reaching orgasm because she never gets to the all-important plateau phase.)

If you want fulfilling sex, it really is important to enjoy the journey as well as the destination. Orgasm may, or may not, be the ultimate goal, but how you get there and what you do along the way are what makes love making wonderful or tedious. Here are some ideas to help you enjoy love making:

- Give yourself plenty of time. Trying to make love when you know you are pushed for time is a recipe for disaster. Try making 'love dates' in your diary when you can be together without interruption for at least an hour. It is worth putting other things aside in order to do this.

- Choose a room where you will be private. It may be useful to put locks on doors sometimes so you can bar the way to being accidentally discovered. If you have small children, this may seem harsh but I am not asking you to prevent them ever coming into your bedroom at all, just to occasionally value your love life more than their access to you at all times. Make love when they are asleep if at all possible. Of course, if there are safety issues, these should prevail over privacy.

- Make the room attractive. If you want to make love but have to clear a load of dirty washing or make the bed before you can start, all the romance will seem dead before you begin. When you next decorate the room think about which colours feel warm and erotic. Use lighting shades that give a room a rosy glow (rather than blues and greens). Candles and scented oil burners offer a flattering light for love making.

- Consider if you always want to be undressed at the start of love making. Wearing silky underwear or a nightdress can be a turn-on at the start of love making. A satin slip or silk boxer shorts slide sensually over the skin as you caress one another.

- Use good-quality massage oil to caress one another. A good alternative to this is a light dusting of talcum powder as this also aids your hands in sliding over the skin. (Do not try the two together or you will end up with a sticky mess!) Caress and stroke your partner's body all over. Pay as much attention to their whole body as to their genitals or breasts. Take your time. Ask your partner what they would like you to do and test out different kinds of touching – teasing and soft or firm and massaging.

- Use your mouth and lips to kiss, lick and touch your partner all over. Favourite areas for lip arousal are the neck, the backs of legs and the crook of the arm as well as the erogenous zones of nipples and genitals. Be guided by your partner's response. Do more of what they enjoy! Do not forget to ask your partner to return the compliment.

- Spend plenty of time kissing and cuddling. Let yourself relax into the sensation of pleasure as you embrace. Some people feel tense at the start of love making because they regard it as a performance that they have to get right. Love making is more like an art form. What you produce will be different every time and is valuable, whatever the outcome.

- Consider bathing or showering together before making love or use the bathroom as a venue for sex. The combination of water, shower crème and slippery skin is highly erotic. If you choose not to actually make love in the bathroom, a warm bath, together or alone, before sex will help you relax and feel in a sensual mood.

Sex play

If you shift your attitude towards sex from performance to play you will need some 'toys' to help you really enjoy love making. By 'toys' I mean some items to have nearby and some techniques to help you get the most out of your love making. Here is a list of things you might like to keep in your 'love cupboard' and some ideas to extend your love-making pleasure.

- **Lubricant**. Different kinds of lubricant can be used for different parts of the body. A good-quality allover massage oil is very useful and can be bought from most chemists and beauty counters. Try The Body Shop for delicious scents. You will also need a lubricant specifically designed to apply to the vaginal opening and labia, penis and testicles. Try water-, silicone- and gel-based lubricants to decide which you prefer. Water and silicone lubricants most closely resemble natural lubrication. Gel-based lubricants (KY Jelly, for instance) are thicker and stickier, but do have more staying power. Even if you produce plenty of natural lubricant during love play, extra lubrication can add to the sensuous quality of sex. If you are a post-menopausal woman, or recently had a baby, lubricants can make potentially uncomfortable sex much pleasanter and enjoyable. Ordinary olive oil is also useful as a lubricant, if a little messier than the branded lubricants available in the shops and on-line. Keep a towel to hand to mop up any unintended spills!

- **Silk scarves and/or satin or silk underwear**. You may think I am about to stray into the area of push-up bras and stockings, but I am not. Sexy underwear, often a turn-on to men, is mostly seen by women as scratchy and uncomfortable. (But if you enjoy it, there is no reason why you should not wear it.) I am thinking of the softer satin and silk night clothing that is sold in most high-street stores. Caressing your partner through silky material can be a wonderful experience for both of you. It also means that men get to play as well. Caressing your partner under and over a silky pair of boxer shorts can feel wickedly erotic. Use the silk scarves to drape over one another's bodies. Run them slowly over the full length of the body, wrap them around your hands as you caress each other or spread them over your partner before you lie on top of them.

- **Pillows and cushions**. You are very likely to have pillows on your bed and cushions in the lounge, but perhaps have never viewed them as sex aids before! Place a pillow under the woman's buttocks before attempting penetration in the face-to-face position. This tilts the pelvis, giving her deep but comfortable penetration. It can also stimulate the G Spot, situated in the front wall of the vagina, near the entrance. (The G Spot is a contested part of female anatomy. Some women find direct stimulation of this area of the vagina highly arousing. In others it just causes a strong desire to go to the loo! If it works for you, enjoy it. If not, do not bother with it.) A pillow placed under your or your partner's bottom during oral sex is also an aid as you can then concentrate on the appropriate area without whatever you are lying on getting in the way. If you have a cylinder-shaped pillow this can aid rear entry positions. Place it under the woman's lower chest or abdomen to elevate the vaginal entrance. Or put it behind the neck so that the woman or man's head is tilted back in face to-face-positions. This is reputed to increase sensation during orgasm.

- **Feather boas, fans (electric or otherwise) and fur fabric**. Cheap feather boas can be purchased from lots of high-street stores and make a wonderful aid to love making. Slowly drag the feathers over the whole body, or wear it as you caress your partner. The tantalising movement of the feathers over the skin can be highly arousing. Fan your partner with a paper fan, or hold an electric fan above their naked body. The movement of the air over the skin, especially if the room is already warm, feels delicious. If you have fur gloves or fur fabric in the house, try caressing your partner with them. A fur bed-spread or rug is great to roll about on when making love (with the added bonus of allowing you to feel as if you are in a James Bond film!)

- **A vibrator**. If you think all vibrators are basically plastic willies you need to check out the new generation of vibrators available. Some are designed to suit a woman's anatomy more accurately, concentrating on the clitoris and labia rather than the less responsive internal area of the vagina. Look for natural shapes and contours. Some also fit on a finger so that the man or woman can apply vibration directly to the clitoris. Visit www.emotionalbliss.com for this kind of vibe. A good vibrator can improve arousal and sexual excitement and should be seen as a fun extra to love making rather than the only way to reach orgasm quickly as this can add to the goal-orientated attitude you want to avoid. Men can also benefit from a shaped vibrator as it can be placed under the testes to produce pleasant and stimulating sensations.

Techniques that increase pleasure

- Take your time. Avoid rushed sex, as it can often be a disappointment. Spend lots of time on kissing and caressing one another all over before racing to intercourse.

- Try arousing one another with hands and lips until close to orgasm. As your excitement mounts, pause so that the arousal level dies down a little. Then resume arousal. Do this two or three times. This slight pause will extend the length of your arousal, leading to extremely intense orgasms.

- During stimulation, put your hand over your partner's to guide the pressure and movement you would like. You can also ask your partner to put his/her hand over yours to demonstrate how you like to be touched.

- Try having sex that does not always end in intercourse. Mutual stimulation to orgasm, without penetration, is not only often extremely exciting and fulfilling, but also teaches you both what turns your partner on, allowing for sex that feels natural and bonding.

- Stroke neglected areas of the body. Try gently touching the face, neck and hair of your partner. Offer to give a foot or hand massage. These intimate caresses feel especially tender and warm.

- Take responsibility for your own sexual pleasure. Expecting a partner to know how to arouse you without communicating what you like is unfair and prevents your sex life from developing. Do not be afraid to offer words and sounds of praise and pleasure when they get it right. If things do not go so well, avoid barking commands in the middle of love making!. Take their hand and guide them (see above) or say 'I love it when you kiss me there' or 'Touch me here'.

Asking for sex

Do you feel that you are sometimes out of step with each other sexually? Maybe just one person tends to initiate sex or you both wait for the other to ask. This situation can sometimes lead to frustration and hurt. It often happens out of habit. Perhaps one partner always asked for sex when the relationship began so that an expectation develops that is hard to break.

A quick-fix solution is to arrange dates in your diary when you will put time aside for love making. This may sound rather clinical, but if you can get over the initial strangeness it can work really well. You may not always make love, but a precious hour or two that you know you have both put aside to be close avoids the disagreements about who asks for love making and if one or the other is in the mood. You may enjoy a cuddle, a massage, a moment of peace listening to some music, or make love. Whatever you do will enhance your love life. You are worth the trouble to arrange this meeting. Do not put everything else before your intimate life together.

Fulfilling and rewarding sex is not about how often you make love. It is about what you do and how you feel during love making. Arguments about frequency often occur when the content of love making is poor. Couples can feel that if they did it more the problem with content would somehow be sorted out as if by magic. But this is not the case. Creating a good sex life takes effort and sensitive attention from both of you. If you are willing to approach your sex life with an open mind and a sense of adventure, it will stay fresh and alive. A creative and loving sex life helps to maintain a happy day-to-day relationship. The organisation 'Relate' has found that its sex therapy programme not only improves the sex life of people attending, but also their everyday life. Quality, not quantity, is what makes a happy sex life.

8
GET YOUR WORK/LIFE BALANCE RIGHT

As a counsellor and therapist I am often asked what difficulty is having the most impact on a couple in the new millennium. My reply is creating a successful work/life balance. This is a brand new phenomenon. Until this generation, men and women tended to occupy separate niches. Women did one thing, men another. Childcare was primarily carried out by women, paid work by men. If women did work, their job was seen as less significant than that of men (even if it was of the same kind) and less well paid. If men cared for children, it was viewed as odd and probably because his wife was ill or otherwise incapable. With the revolution in attitudes to gender roles that has taken place since the 1960s, including the equality of rights and pay for women, these views have been swept aside. It is now accept-able for a man to care for his children and his female partner to go to work. This has meant that men and women have more freedom and more choice than ever before in how they order their lives together. It is good news for couples everywhere.

But there are some drawbacks. When roles were clearly demarcated men and women knew where they stood. Each had their area of 'expertise' and this allowed individuals to feel safe. It was restricting and suffocating for many people but it also gave a sense of belonging that had value. Women supported other women; men had a sense of identification with other men, often through their employment. Life was ordered and predictable.

But today everything is different. Each couple who get together today will have to work out what roles they will fulfil in the relationship. Will they both work? Or just one? Who will cook, clean, organise childcare or take the car to the garage? When circumstances change, will these roles remain the same? Life is also much faster, with new technologies to assimilate. Our grandparents and great-grandparents had longer to adjust to change. Now we have to grapple with the latest PC programs, new styles of mobile phones and computers in cars several times a year, never mind over a lifetime! It is as if each couple has to re-invent the wheel for themselves when they decide to commit. This is exciting and fun, but also stressful. It demands excellent communication and negotiation skills alongside a willingness to be open to new ways of approaching decisions.

Making Assumptions

The first problem that often strikes a couple when they get together and want to sort out domestic arrangements is that they make assumptions about what should happen. They assume their partner will want certain things or do things the same way they do. This is dangerous as assumptions are borne out of guesswork and guessing inaccurately what is important to your partner can cause rows.

Here is a list of things that have to be done regularly in a living-together relationship. Tick the column that represents the person you think should do the task or whose responsibility it should be. You can tick both columns if you think it should always be a shared responsibility. Do this separately from your partner and then compare lists. Do not let them see what you have ticked first.

Task	Me	My Partner
Cooking		
Vacuuming and dusting		
Washing clothes		
Ironing		
Taking the car for MOT		
Cutting the grass/ gardening		
Cleaning the toilet and bath		
Changing the sheets on the bed		
Washing up/using dishwasher		
Organising builder/plumber/ electrician, etc., when needed		
Paying the mortgage/ rent		
Paying bills		
Shopping for food		
Shopping for household items		
Paid work to support the family/relationship		

Task	Me	My Partner
Buying gifts for friends and relatives for birthdays and Christmas		
Arranging evenings out		
Putting petrol in the car		
Organising childcare (babysitters/childminders)		
Taking children to school		
Picking children up from school		
Taking children to after-school activities		
Inviting friends for shared social events		
Arranging social events for the two of you		
Deciding who watches which TV channel		
Choosing a video/DVD to watch		

If you have ticked both columns for most of these you are doing well. But perhaps the most interesting part of this exercise is to look at those you hesitated over or only ticked one column on. Why did you take this decision? And how did you decide what to do? Do you feel resentful about doing the tasks you do and does your list look lopsided, with one of you doing more than the other does? Or are you content with how the list is divided?

Most people who complete these kinds of list have never discussed why they do the things they do. They may have decided that it was up to them as the man or woman, because they were the first person home from work or because it is how their parents organised things, for instance. It is rare for a couple to sit down and talk about why tasks are undertaken the way they are. Sometimes if this kind of conversation takes place it can rapidly become uncomfortable because some basic assumptions have been made that one or other partner has never been party to. If domestic tasks are done and both partners are happy about it, you may never have to talk about this at all. The problem is that things rarely stay the same for long. Take the example of the couple where the woman does the majority of the housework while her partner works in paid employment. If he is made redundant and she takes on work to pay the bills she may feel resentful and upset if her partner refuses to undertake the housework, regarding it as her job, not his. Knowing how to talk about your own work/life balance can help you iron out potential problems in the future.

Talking about your list

Are you gender biased?

As you look at your list, think about if you have divided up tasks because you think a man or a woman should do them. You may think that this attitude went out with the ark, but many couples unconsciously still divide tasks into his and hers. This may work for you, but it might need challenging if either of you feels they got their share by default rather than discussion.

Are you reward biased?

Housework you do for yourself is not paid. One of you may decide that, because they work for money, this is their full contribution to the couple. If you are not in paid work, they may expect you to undertake tasks in order to compensate for not working in a paid position. This situation is a very common assumption and is often met by women who have left work to have children. Their partner makes a set of assumptions about what will happen while the woman is at home with a new baby without telling her this is the case! So housework becomes a contribution in lieu of money. Couples who do this can often make it work well because it feels fair in the situation they find themselves in. But if it is unexpected or unexamined, you can both feel short-changed if things go wrong. A similar scenario can occur if one of you works part-time and the other works full-time. An assumption may be made that the part-timer will do the majority of the housework. Never expect this kind of arrangement without discussing the implications.

Are you task blind?

Nobody likes doing things they find frustrating or irritating. This is true for any domestic challenge. Perhaps you undertake the things you do because you hate washing-up, cleaning the loo or DIY. This is an avoidance that many people encounter. You may even do lots of helpful things in an effort to make up for not doing the things you loathe. But your partner may never understand this unless you explain.

Are you afraid?

Do you know you avoid certain activities because you have never learnt how to do them? Or perhaps you hate taking the car to the garage because you do not understand the terms the mechanic uses, or making dinner arrangements with friends because you are shy? As you look back at your list you will probably find some of these there. Others of this kind include avoiding using the computer because you are unsure of what to do or the washing machine because no one has shown you what buttons to push. You may not think of these as things you feel nervous about. Instead, you may have rationalised the issue by telling yourself that your partner enjoys them or has more knowledge. This is OK if they are also happy with this idea. But if you experience a mismatch of who does what, you are likely to fall out over these minor irritations. If this is a serious problem, you should learn how to use machines in the home, even if only at a basic level. After all, if anything happened to your partner you would need to know how to operate the washing machine or video timer.

Divide up your life

Here is an easy way to start you thinking about how to manage your life together. Using the list, make three marks in your column. One mark for tasks you like (yes, some people like ironing!) Now mark those you would do if you had to, but perhaps currently avoid. Lastly, mark those you really hate. Try to be even-handed and honest. Now ask your partner to do the same thing. Once you have both filled out your list you should end up with some overlapping areas. Now start trading. Pick the hated tasks first. Ask your partner if they love any of them and would take them straight away. Offer to take on a hated task of theirs to compensate. Next, look at your mutual 'could do' lists. If necessary, do some trading of tasks according to the strength of your feelings. If you have lots of shared 'love it' items, you may need to do a straightforward 'you take half and I will take half'. If you have a lot of shared 'hate it', items you may need to agree to regularly swap tasks to reduce the annoyance factor. Agree to trade tasks once a month so that nothing seems too onerous for too long. Once you have used this system you can review it if your situation changes.

When work takes over

Many couples feel that work is gradually invading their life. No longer does it stay neatly at the office or factory, but can haunt time with a partner or family. If you commute, you may have noticed that lots of people spend travelling time working on laptop computers or making extensive calls on their mobile phones. They are likely to continue these activities at home, checking e-mails or calling colleagues long into the evening. The working day can often start at 7 a.m. on the train and finish at 10 p.m. while sitting on the sofa at home, even if the official hours are 9 to 5 in the office. Statistics show that 1,000,000 people in the UK work more than 60 hours a week. If you do not actually bring work home, you may find your mind preoccupied with what is going on at work or worrying about some aspect of your job after working hours. All of this work concern can eat away at your relationship. Instead of enjoying time together you may be so preoccupied that you talk about nothing else or are so tired that your relationship slides down your list of priorities and is neglected. Here are some ideas to help you put work in its place so you can have a better relationship together.

- When you come home from work, change your clothes and give yourself half an hour of quiet time before tackling home-based chores. Share a cup of tea or a chat before getting on with the rest of the day. If you commute, try to use the time as a watershed before returning. If you are driving, play some relaxing music. Remember that your partner will also have had his or her experiences in the day. Be sensitive to where they are rather than just what you have been doing.

- Agree a cut-off time for talking about work. Decide you will only talk about work until 6 or 7 p.m. or until the evening meal is eaten, for instance. Then fill the time with anything that is important to you or doing something you enjoy.

- Avoid checking e-mails or taking phone calls once you are home. It is tempting to check up on what is going on to allay anxiety about work, but your partner may begin to wonder if you are married to the PC or mobile phone instead of him or her!

- Practise giving each other concentrated attention time. Ten or fifteen minutes of attention are better than an hour broken by phone calls or dealing with paperwork. A good rule of thumb is to listen twice as much as you speak. In this way you can pay attention to what your partner is saying and think through any action that you wish to take.

- If you work from home, it is crucial to have a separate place for all your work-related items. Avoid placing a PC or work phone/fax in a family space, or covering the kitchen table in files. Not only will you have trouble keeping track of what you are doing but also the family will find it difficult to avoid messing up your work material. This blurring of the line between home and work can cause arguments so avoid it if at all possible.

Why work can grip you

When work gets a grip on your life to the detriment of your relationship, it is helpful to think through why you are spending so much time on work. For some people it is linked to where they gain their self-esteem.

Think of it like this. You may be a 'pushed' or a 'pulled' person. If you are a 'pushed' type, you are likely to worry about getting things wrong and feel fearful of what will happen if you do not dot every i and cross every t. If this sounds like you, you probably spend lots of time at work or bring work home in case you are discovered to be lacking in some way. Other people are 'pulled' by work. They aspire to promotion or some other reward from work – increased pay or prestige. If this is you, you may spend hours working in order to achieve these dreamed-of goals. From either position, your partner may not understand exactly what is going on. They may only observe you working all hours and feel second place. If you are a 'pushed' type, work on increasing your self-confidence rather than driving yourself into the ground by obsessively checking everything you do. Learn to delegate and limit how much you take on. Talk to your partner about how you feel about work and gain their encouragement to trust that you do your job well. If you are the 'pulled' type, allow yourself to reflect on how important your rewards for the job really are. You may want the latest car, but your partner probably wants your time and attention more. Cut back on work for reward and you could find your relationship more satisfying.

If you are working long hours and feel afraid to go home, work has become your escape. Reflect on what the anxiety is about. Are you arguing more? Is your partner critical of you and what you do? Has your partner let you down in some way? In this situation it is common for the person to gradually gain more of their self-esteem from work. After all, if you were praised for your actions at work but moaned at for what you did at home, where would you want to spend most of your time? Work as an escape can seem appealing. If you spend lots of time there, and have your own space, it can feel more like home than home! In addition, if you have friends at work who you feel connected to because of shared work goals, you may feel more understood by them than your partner. But ultimately your connection to your partner is the one that is likely to stand the test of time. Friendships made while you are at work usually have a slender connection because they are, by necessity, woven from work issues. This means that if work ends, or you move on, it is possible that your friendships will finish. You may know the phenomenon yourself. You vow to see each other once you are working in different places, but a year on from moving offices you only occasionally see one or two die-hard mates that have survived your relocation. By contrast, your relationship covers more than just a small part of your life, providing support and pleasure in much more than work. It is worth investing time and effort in keeping it alive and satisfying so that your attitude towards work retains a sense of perspective.

Working with a partner

The number of couples working together has grown enormously in the last ten years. Self-employment and small businesses are increasing as old-style firms, where people might have worked for fifty years, decline. This allows for creative opportunities that many couples relish. The chance to share working as a partnership on a project that fascinates them can boost togetherness and intimacy. But it can also cause difficulties. Working together can cause tension and may mean that work 'bleeds' into couple and family life so that you feel as if every conversation is work related. Work and everyday life can feel fogged. This may be OK when you are founding a new business, especially if you are very busy and excited about the prospects ahead. But if you are still talking about work as you climb into bed, you will gradually feel that you are living to work rather than working to live.

Try these tips to help you manage working with your life partner:

- Behave as if you are professionals, not lovers! Draw up a contract (with legal help if necessary) so that you both know where you stand if things do not go according to plan. Study Company Law and decide who is responsible if the business fails and what this might mean to your shared finances or collateral.

- Never leave money management to just one partner. Make sure you both agree on strategies for the business and monitor cash in and out together. If you have special responsibilities that the other has little to do with, keep him or her up to date by writing notes and keeping up-to-date files they can read.

- Appoint staff together. It may seem easy to give jobs to family and friends, but take into account any problems that could emerge if they take you for granted or if you fall out with them.

- If you begin to feel that you are taking on more work than your partner, talk to them about what is happening. Resentments over one partner feeling taken for granted are very common in family businesses so check out what is going on regularly. Never make assumptions that your partner will do something if you have forgotten.

- Take all the holidays and 'down' time you can. Make sure you have weekends together if possible. Even if you are on a budget, a week away from the business will relax you so you are ready for the fray on your return. Not making good use of your leisure time (and you should definitely have at least some!) is a recipe for stress and exhaustion. No one can run a business when they are worn out, so regular breaks will help you succeed rather than fall at the first hurdle.

- Sort out childcare and domestic help (if you need them) together. Never assume that this is something you or your partner will do automatically. Talk through how you will manage this area of your life and cost out what taking on extra help will mean to your finances.

Hidden problems

When both partners in a relationship work there are sometimes taboo subjects that hardly ever get mentioned but that can have a serious impact on your work/life balance. Read the following to see if you can identify with any of these hidden issues.

Your partner thinks you should not be in the job you have chosen

If your career is a dangerous one (armed forces, fire service, police, etc.), it is possible that your partner will feel torn in supporting you. They may want you to do well but fear that you will be hurt, or even killed, in your job. They may find this hard to say to you but could make it clear in other ways. They may drop hints that they want you to change careers or take a desk job rather than being on the front line.

A variation on this is that your job is middle of the road but your partner thinks you should aspire to better things, either because they think you are more able or because he or she would like you to make more money. If you get enough hints or nagging about this, it can undermine your confidence because you may think you should also want to improve your lot even if you are perfectly happy as you are.

Dealing with this issue can be tricky because your partner may not come straight out and say what is on their mind. It is useful to occasionally explain how you feel about your job – what it does for you mentally, emotionally and physically, why you have chosen the role you have and why you intend to stay in it. Do not wait for a row for this to emerge. Drop it into conversation in a natural way. Avoid the temptation to always tell him or her when things have gone wrong at work. Couples often concentrate on telling each other the problems at work in order to get support after a hard day, but neglect to mention the other days when things were great. Share good work days and achievements as much as possible so that he or she can see how important your job is to you. Be assertive, but not aggressive, and your partner will see how important the job you have is to you, not the job they would like you to have.

Your partner earns more than you or has a job with greater responsibility

Some couples struggle with earning disparity. This is most likely to occur when the lower-paid partner is also unhappy with their job. For them, the contrast between career misery and a well-paid and satisfied partner can usher in a sense of jealousy and resentment. He or she may experience a tearing of loyalties, feeling ashamed of their emotions but unable to stifle their real sense of feeling unequal to a partner who is succeeding in their choice of career.

The best way to deal with this problem, and avoid the issue festering between the two of you, is to be up front with your partner. Explain how you are feeling. It is important to differentiate between your resentment caused by your own unhappiness at work and your feelings towards your partner's role. If you are dissatisfied at work, this is not because your partner is doing well. Their success merely emphasises your own experience. Never blame them for something you need to tackle, for example, saying 'you make me feel useless' or 'it's all so easy for you'. If you notice this attitude creeping in, you need to take action. Get some career guidance or talk to your partner about what you would really like to do. If you are a factory worker but wish you were a potter, maybe they would be willing to support you while you retrain. Or perhaps you could improve your prospects by training in a different aspect of your work. There are always more options than seem immediately obvious. Make a list and talk it through with your partner.

Sometimes this kind of resentment is based on gender. This attitude is changing, but there are still some couples who encounter the 'she should not earn more than him' myth. If you are a man who feels it is your role to be the traditional bread-winner, it can seem quite a challenge if your female partner begins to earn more or has a more responsible job than you. If you recognise yourself in this picture, think about where this idea has come from. Is it from your parents? Did you have a dad who took the same line? Or do you think men should be regarded as 'head of the household' because this is how your mum treated your dad? If this seems possible, it is time to challenge this out-of-date notion. It stunts the personal and general development of men and women to suggest that they should occupy very particular roles. Plus, if you are busy defending your right to be the most important or best wage earner, you may be denying yourself the opportunity to do other things, such as nurturing your children or exploring leisure pursuits you would enjoy. Power struggles of this kind often indicate an imbalance in the relationship in other areas so it could be worth trying to work out why you are playing 'one-upmanship' games in this way. Low self-confidence or feelings that you were always the one who lost out to brothers or sisters can play a part in this way of thinking and behaving.

Another common scenario in this area is when one partner takes time away from work while the other partner remains at work. The most common reason is that the woman has had a baby and is taking temporary or permanent leave from work. After the immediate excitement of the birth and settling down at home, many women experience feelings of a change in their place in society. From managing a team at work to washing Babygros can seem a big step down. If your partner continues to do well at work, you may feel as if you have lost your role. If this happens to you, remember that having a child is a huge emotional change in life. You may be centring your feelings about becoming a mother on work issues as a way of managing your emotions. This is because the responsibility of parenting can seem overwhelming in the early months of mothering. Try to allow yourself to lean on your partner for support – both emotionally and financially – rather than fight to feel you must be superwoman, capable of doing everything at once. You need several months to adjust to the situation and a little dependence now is OK. Hanging on to your desire to match your partner in work indicates you are feeling unsure about being a parent. This is natural and normal. Every new mother or father feels unsure about their new role. Instead of fighting this feeling try allowing yourself to acknowledge its truth. If you intend to return to work, allow yourself to have a phased return, with several part days, before returning full-time. In this way, you can cope with the transition gradually rather than slam straight into work again, creating another seismic shift in your life after giving birth.

Your family and/or friends disapprove of your choice of work

On the surface this may not seem to have much impact on your relationship. You could feel that this is a problem your family and friends should deal with rather than you or your partner. But the disapproval of those who support you in other ways can sometimes cause difficulties. For example, if you want to work on a smallholding in Wales but your parents think you should use your law degree they partly funded, you may face years of defending your position. Your family may see your partner as a way of getting to you so that he or she finds himself or herself shielding you from criticism. If they have any misgivings at all, your family's attacks could eventually cause him or her to feel unhappy about your choice. Alternatively, he or she may feel you would both be better with no contact, thereby causing a rift in the family that you will regret in time.

In managing this issue I hope it goes without saying that your partner must be in agreement (or at the very least tolerant of) your decision to change or enter a different profession to the one that was expected of you. If he or she is also resentful and miserable, your relationship will suffer alongside the problems you may face with your family. To bolster your confidence make a list of the reasons why you have decided to take up the job you have chosen. If you feel sure of why you are doing that job, you will be able to reason with your family and partner more effectively. This exercise is also useful if you feel a strong compulsion to do something different but you are unable to assess why you feel this way. Writing a 'reasons for' list can act as a diagnostic, helping you to make sense of your thinking and feeling. You could also add a 'reasons against' list to add balance.

Occasionally, the decision to work in a job that your family or partner does not understand is caused by a sense of vocation. You may want to be a vicar when everyone else you know is atheist or agnostic so that, as far as they are concerned, your faith comes out of the blue, or you may want to work in an aid agency in a dangerous part of the world. If you want your family, friends and partner to stay on your side, you must explain very carefully why you feel called to do this work. They may still oppose you but they will realise how important this work is to you and, hopefully, eventually support you in your vocation.

Achieving a work/life balance is not easy in a busy lifestyle. But if you can achieve a healthy balance you will reap the benefits of feeling in control rather than out of control. Talking through the ideas in this chapter will allow you both to explore how you can manage your work and home life together so that you give appropriate attention to each when you need to.

9

KEEP A FLEXIBLE ATTITUDE

Most relationships are built on a bedrock of rules that are laid down during the early months and years of being together. The interesting thing about these rules is that they are often invisible supports. They become so much a part of your life together that you may never notice them once they are established. It is rather like a building that is constructed around a network of pillars and struts. Once the brickwork goes on, the main supports are only visible if you have to do some repair work and remove the outer cladding.

This can be a good thing, as constantly testing the base your relationship is constructed on can be a sign that you are unsure of where you stand. If you find yourself asking lots of questions or demanding your partner explains himself or herself over and over again, you may be insecure about the relationship in general. But blindly accepting that the way things have always been is how they will be in the future is extremely dangerous. If you set your partnership in concrete at an early stage it will soon be a fossil.

Research on what makes a relationship likely to succeed suggests two things. The first is the ability to talk about anything. The second – the emotional yoga of relationships – is to maintain a flexible attitude to the future, and allows for you to always adapt to whatever life throws at you. If you can keep your shared approach supple and lively, your relationship will not petrify but feel interesting no matter how long you have been together.

!

So how can you tell if your relationship is a fossil or alive and kicking? Look at the lists below and tick those you agree with. Then read the response at the bottom of the lists.

Set in stone?

1 I often feel bored in my relationship

2 I sometimes feel constricted by my relationship

3 Questioning how we do things can cause arguments

4 I often feel nervous about doing something new as a couple

5 We hardly ever talk about what is important to us

6 I would find it hard to explain why we do things the way we do

7 My partner does not like change

8 I do not like change

9 We do some things because they suited us when we first got together

10 Routine is very important to us

Work in progress?

1 I rarely have time to feel bored with my relationship

2 I feel free to be myself in my relationship

3 We like to look at different options when we make choices together

4 I usually feel confident about new things we do together

5 We talk a lot about what is important to us

6 I could easily explain how and why we made a particular decision

7 My partner embraces change

8 I enjoy new things

9 We frequently review how we do things

10 Our routines can be challenged without too much difficulty

Set in stone?

If you agreed with more than six of these statements, you may have a relationship that is pretty inflexible. You probably started out full of ideas about how the partnership would work only to find that you have made these into inflexible rules rather than useful guidelines along the way. You have discovered that although a relationship based on rigid rules can feel safe and secure it can also make you feel bored and trapped. Part of you longs to be freer while another part fears putting a foot wrong. There may be good reasons why you are in this position. If the relationship has been through rough times – often money worries or problems with your children – you may have clung on to what felt safe. But this can only last for a while before you begin to experience feelings of suffocation. Read the rest of this chapter to get some new ideas about how to create a relationship that is less restrictive.

Work in progress?

If you agreed with more than six of these statements you are in a relationship that is open to new ideas and ways of doing things. You may have learnt to challenge each other from the start or had to find a way of doing this that allowed you to feel comfortable with each other. You have learnt how to talk and listen to one another with respect. It is likely that you encourage one another to explore new ways of doing things and that this has given your relationship a liveliness that is appealing to others as well as to one another. Your flexibility enables you to get over difficult times as you are constantly searching for new ways to deal with problems that arise. This is all good for the future but you may still learn some new tricks from reading the rest of this chapter.

Unearthing your buried rules

Discovering what is supporting your relationship is helpful as you improve flexibility in your partnership. Some kinds of foundations are helpful as they support and hold the relationship safely while still allowing for development at other times. Some are shaky and rusty, only holding on because the relationship itself has not altered for so long. Deciding what state your foundations are in is helpful because you can either decide to change only a little or undertake a complete renovation so that you are ready for the unknown future ahead of you. Here is a brief exercise you can try alone or with your partner.

Imagine yourself writing a contract that describes how your relationship was founded. What would you include and why? What do you think of as immovable and what has been negotiable? Here is an example to get you started.

This contract describes our relationship when it was founded and is written by Tom and Helen.

Clause 1 We agree to be faithful to one another for as long as we are together. If one of us is unfaithful we will split up.

Clause 2 We agree to split the household costs equally. Helen will live in Tom's flat and pay for the bills and food. Tom will pay the rent and sundry other costs while we are together.

Clause 3 Helen agrees to support Tom emotionally while he finishes his training as an accountant. Tom agrees to support Helen emotionally as she moves into a full-time nursing career.

Clause 4 We agree to maintain our favourite leisure pursuits such as going to the cinema and hill walking.

To be read carefully:

Clause 5 Tom agrees to never mention Helen's former fiancé and to avoid behaving in the same way as him. Helen agrees to be sensitive to Tom's close relationship to his widowed mother. Helen agrees to put up with visiting Tom's sister, even though she does not like her. We will spend Christmas with our families. Our sex life will continue as it began.

Helen and Tom's contract looks, on the surface, as if it has a lot to recommend it. There is a mixture of emotional and practical support and a sense of wanting to preserve the relationship as interesting and lively. But every contract has some small print. As you may guess, these are issues that Tom and Helen may never have voiced to each other but were part of the unspoken building blocks of their relationship. What is your guess about the hidden issues in this relationship? It looks as though Helen has suffered some unhappiness about her former fiancé and wanted Tom to behave very differently. This has probably influenced Clause 1, so we might surmise that her ex was unfaithful to Helen. Tom has a close relationship to his mother that Helen was warned of right from the start. Helen was also asked to take Tom's family at face value and not complain, even if she is not keen on a member of it. Neither has accepted that their sexual relationship was likely to change as time goes on.

Now look at *your* contract. What is in your clauses? Think about why you put them in the order you did. Now consider what might be in your own small print. Has this influenced your relationship a lot or a little? Have you kept to your contract or changed it as circumstances have dictated? Helen and Tom could have found themselves in hot water if the small print became more important as the years went by. For example, what if Tom's mother took up more and more of his time as she grew older, pushing Helen into second place? Or if Helen became overly possessive of Tom in case he let her down, as her previous fiancé had done? This is the problem with inflexibility – it can lock you into doing things the same way forever.

There is an instructive myth about this kind of behaviour. An ancient tribe taught their children everything they needed to know about living in their environment. It was a cold country and the children needed to know how to hunt animals in order to make fur coats and where to find the nutritious plants that survived the ice and snow. Then the climate changed. It became much warmer. Fur coats were too hot and edible plants multiplied so that searching became redundant. What was needed was to know how to weave loose cool clothing and to learn how to catch fish in the warmer water. But the elders felt that the children should continue to have a traditional education and learn about fur hunting and plants grown in ice. The children carried on trying to do what the elders told them but gradually the tribe began to suffer. They grew ill, as they were unable to take advantage of the changed climate. The elders stubbornly insisted that their methods were correct. Only when the last few members were left alive did the tribe realise that their adherence to the old ways had destroyed them. Then they took action and learnt the skills they needed to survive.

Many couples behave in this way. They stick rigidly to one particular way of doing things when the reason for it has long gone. They may divide the household chores in a way that suited them when they first got together, avoiding acquiring the knowledge they may need if anything happens to their partner.

Here are some issues that couples often create rules around. See if any of them sound like topics you know you have hidden rules about:

Money

Money can be at the root of lots of small-print clauses. Who earns it, how it is spent and saved and what it means to each partner. You may have good reason for saving every penny at twenty-five but is it still applicable at forty-five? Spending priorities can also be a source of confusion if your original contract says 'we will buy a new car every three years' but find the cost is too great and you need the money for something else. This is especially true if one of you tends to want to save and the other to spend. Unspoken contracts can sometimes force one or other into agreeing to spend or save for years ahead.

Sex

You may not think of sex as being part of a contract but how you behave sexually when you begin your intimate life can affect what you expect in the future. The most common thing that happens is that the quantity of sex declines and one partner feels more upset or surprised about this than the other. This is a natural phenomenon in couple relationships, but if your contract says 'sex will always be five times a week', you may find you feel tense and awkward over love making as time progresses. It is also possible that you have contract clauses that your partner knows nothing about! For example, you may have very small print that says 'sex is important to me because it is a way of expressing my affection. Without it I do not know if I am loved'. If your partner does not realise they signed up to this, you could be open to months and years of misunderstanding when your partner is too tired for sex or there is a forced separation between you – perhaps because of work – and sex is not possible.

Family and friends

How you both feel about your family and friends, their influence on you and your sense of the importance of family is important as you decide who will support your relationship. Most people have unique views of their family – how close they feel to them or why they behave the way they do. This can become mixed up with what they expect of you. How he or she responds to their parents may be what they expect from you. If his or her mother is cool and contained, for instance, they may expect the same behaviour from you. Or if his or her father is thoughtful and supportive, they may expect the same of you.

This is especially true if you are the same sex as their mother or father.

You may also find that things like visiting family and friends are written in your personal contract. Contact with your partner's or your own family may be very important or to be avoided at all costs! You could find you had agreed to Sunday lunch with your mother-in-law for the next twenty years without knowing it! Sticking rigidly to an unspoken agreement of this kind can be tough on both of you as your family may come to expect it, leaving you with no way of altering the contract without causing offence. Of course, you may want this kind of agreement, but it can be hard to undertake if you are not aware that it is being set in the first place.

Children and work

I have put these two together because attitudes towards them are often linked. You may actively talk about whether you would like children or assume that this is also a life goal for your partner. If either of you already has children, you are likely to have expectations of your partner that appear on your contract but you never actively speak about. For instance, if you are divorced and have children, you may think your new partner should share in the caring when you have them to stay at weekends. You could just think of this as given – we're together so he or she should want to do this – but all this could change if you have children of your own.

Work can also end up on the contract. How much you do and who is responsible for it. Who gives up work if you have children or arranges the childcare when you go back to work?

These are all contract items that lots of couples have no idea are in the small print of their relationship agreement. Once taken as 'the law' they can take on a mythological life of their own, feeling more like shackles than guidelines you have based your relationship on.

Domestic life

When you first form a relationship it is common for you to divide aspects of domesticity between you. One of you knows how to work the washing machine so they do all the washing, for example. But you need to share your expert knowledge so that your partner can help or take over in a crisis. If your partner has to go away on a trip for a while, it is no good waiting for them to come home to tackle the huge pile of washing caused by your ignorance of all the buttons on the machine! Talk about how things are divided and decide if this is still working for you.

Staying flexible

Successful couples constantly adapt to what life throws at them. They tend to look at the needs of every individual situation rather than try to make each event fit around a way of thinking that is no longer appropriate. Here is how to make your relationship flexible and responsive to different situations.

- *Think about what might be in the building blocks of your relationship*. When you got together did you have a particular attitude to the issue you are facing? Is it still appropriate? For example, if you have always found spending money on expensive holidays difficult because you were trying to support the kids, is it still right to have this approach throughout the whole of your life?

- *Look at each event separately*. If you struggled financially last time one of you changed a job it does not mean it will happen again. Do not react to events as if they are a duplicate of last time. There may be similarities, and you may want to use your learning from these, but always inspect the new situation for differences as well. Use creative approaches to solving new issues. For example, use 'for and against' lists to help you make decisions. Think through each step of an issue, working on what each stage needs to help a situation succeed.

- *Unpack problems.* If you respond to a problem as if you are using your fossilised response, you are likely to take it as a whole. Taking the problem apart can prevent you always reacting in the same way to what seems like a similar problem. For example, if you find you get angry because your teenage stepdaughter is late home every Saturday evening, try to understand why this is happening. Ask her why she is late. Find out who she is with and where she has been. It could be that spending time with a particular friend causes her to be late, or that she missed the bus or ran out of cash. Look at each reason and work out if you could change each of the difficulties. Could you offer to give her and her friend a meal, give her a lift or lend her some money? Tackling the issue in small, bite-size pieces rather than attempting to deal with the problem in one large swallow can make a positive difference.

- *Talk about what you should do.* Making assumptions about what is going to happen in any given situation is the largest cause of stuck thinking. Never guess what your partner thinks, or decide that because you have always done a thing one way that is how it will be forever. Ask your partner for their opinion and offer yours. Look for new ways of seeing things. Try this. Imagine you are in a helicopter flying over the decision you want to make. What can you see as you look down? People who do this often find they see the bigger picture, which helps them to react appropriately to each issue. They are more able to take a wider view so they can form a response that takes everything into account rather than following a well-worn, but not necessarily helpful, path. It can even help to draw a picture of the problem. In this way

A Problem Map

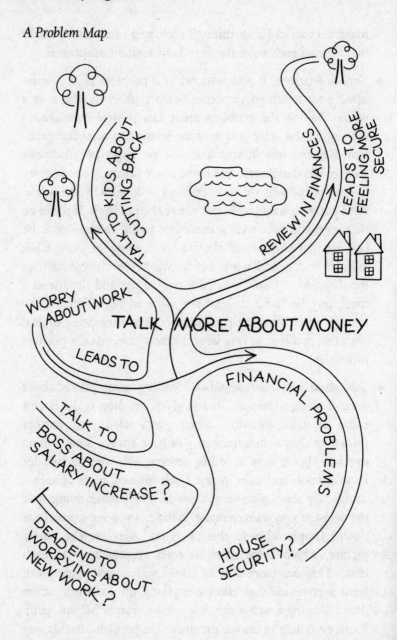

you can see how different elements affect each other. Decision/problem mapping is useful because it will help you make sense of what steps need to be taken and in what order.

- *Think about what would make you happy.* In lots of situations a cautious approach can seem the best way of doing things. But if you want a relationship that sparkles, it is sometimes good to think about what would give you happiness for its own sake. For instance, it may be sensible to plant a vegetable garden (and this could make you happy) but you may need to think of having plants that are not useful but beautiful. Have at least part of your relationship that is for no reason other than to give you pleasure. If you have a boring shopping trip ahead, decide to share a coffee and a bun at 'half time'. Do things that make you laugh and lay down good memories for the future. Your life together should not be about slogging through work or home chores but about celebrating your enjoyment of being together. If you know this is lacking in your relationship, it is time to bring some joy into your life. A little spontaneity can make all the difference.

Flexibility in a relationship can allow you to deal with anything that comes your way. As you become more used to challenging your hidden rules and developing new ways of managing change, you create a practical and emotional 'tool box'. When faced with a decision or problem you can raid your 'tool box' for the best strategy to tackle whatever you need to manage. As time goes by, this way of working and living together will become second nature. You will hardly notice that you live in a flexible style but will reap the benefits of feeling content and happy with your partner.

10

DO NOT BREAK YOUR PROMISES

Whether it is your marriage vows or your agreement to fill the car with petrol, promises matter. If you say you will do something, and your partner is banking on you doing it, letting them down is a signal that you have stopped caring. Many relationships founder because one partner feels they just cannot trust the other one any longer. Be reliable and your relationship will feel strong and secure. If you are trustworthy, your partner will also think twice about disappointing you. Trust is the foundation of any relationship – without it your relationship will feel like a ball and chain rather than a secure base from which to explore life.

Learning to trust

Without trust life would not be possible. Every time you set foot outside the door you trust in a huge army of people to get you through the day. The person who serviced your car, drives your bus or train, maintains the rails or roads, prepares your lunch or sandwich, looks after your bank account, supplies your medicine, and so on, have to be trusted or everything would be so exhausting that no ordinary day could happen. In fact, if you lack this basic level of trust in others, you are likely to be suffering paranoia and classed as having a mental illness. Most people take this kind of trust for granted and hardly ever think about it. Of course, if you are let down (perhaps if you have an accident because someone was not doing their job properly), you will think about whether you trust a situation. Humans have learnt to trust others as part of their socialisation. From the moment we banded together to hunt a wild animal, or allowed others in a tribe to care for our children while we foraged for nuts and berries, we had to develop trust.

In modern life, we learn about trust from the moment that we are born. A new baby gradually realises that when his or her parent or carer leaves them they will return. If he or she cries, they know that they will be fed or changed, cuddled or played with. This is a crucial part of child development. Children who lack this basic parental response often grow up handicapped by the inability to trust others. It can significantly damage his or her ability to make loving relationships in adulthood. It is the most important element of personal development, along with warmth and affection from a parent. As we grow older, appropriate responses also play their part in the development of trust. For example, the good parent allows their child to experiment with new experiences that are appropriate for their age. Allowing a four-year-old to cross a busy road alone is inappropriate, but teaching an eleven-year-old to navigate their way to school across a road allows them to develop self-judgement, paving the way for taking important decisions in later life. Trust is something we gain an understanding of throughout the whole of life. At each stage of life we build on what we have learnt until we feel confident enough to commit ourselves to another.

As you can see, trust takes a long time to develop. This is why it hurts so much if trust is broken. You may think you are just learning to trust a person, but in fact you are bringing in to play everything you learnt about trust over a lifetime. It can feel as if your personal judgement has been wrecked, causing the feeling that you will never be able to make a proper judgement again. Some people who have suffered a breakage of trust feel unable to do the simplest things, such as choosing items in a supermarket. Car accidents, for instance, can cause this response because your trust in your ability to drive, other road users, the car you were driving, and so on, has been broken. Post traumatic stress syndrome is an example of the destruction of trust on a large scale.

Choosing a partner and learning to trust them is part of this continuum of trusting relationships we make during a lifetime. But with a partner you invest a great deal of yourself, your hopes and expectations. This is why it is such an important part of a relationship and can keep you together if understood or split you up if abused.

Your trust roots

How do you know you can trust your partner? You may answer 'I just know'. But it can be useful to think a bit harder about how you came to feel you could trust them. Look at the sentences below and see how you would complete them. It might help to write your answers down.

1   The first moment I knew I could trust my partner was . . .
      What would the end of this sentence look like for you? Would it be because he or she called you when they said they would? Or when they turned down an evening out with the girls/boys to be with you? Or kept a secret you asked them to? Your early experiences of trust with a partner can provide a template for what follows in your partnership. You should also reflect on what gave you the first clues you could trust this man or woman. For example, if you recalled that

they picked you up from work when they promised, even though this involved a long drive, you will know that it was a special effort to help you, indicating your trust in them was well judged. If you asked for something small, such as a promise to call you, and they let you down on several occasions, your sense of trust in them could have been a bit shaky from the start, although this may have been remedied later in the relationship.

2

I first showed my trustworthiness to my partner by . . .

Now think about what you did at the start of the relationship to demonstrate you could be trusted. Did you keep your promises? Were you honest about yourself and your life? Some people start relationships with a little deception. For example, if you met on the Internet, you might say you were a few years younger than your real age or better looking than you think you really are! In the long term this may not matter, but if either of you was economical with the truth at the start, it may have raised questions about trust later in the relationship.

3

I feel I have been able to trust my partner because . . .

What has kept you believing you can trust your partner? Is it because their daily routine and behaviour towards you allows you to feel your trust is validated? For instance, in daily life they keep their promises and do what they say they will do. Seeing things from your point of view is also important because without this ability they may feel able to act without sensitivity towards you. This kind of behaviour can destabilise your trust of him or her.

4

When we have had a problem we demonstrated our trustworthiness to each other by . . .

When a problem hits, the ability to trust a partner can be

crucial. Think back to the last concern you had to tackle togeth-er. How did you know he/she could be trusted? And what did you do to show you could be trusted? For example, if you had to tackle a family problem, perhaps you were able to trust her/him because they listened to you when you were upset, took the action you asked for or helped you manage any fallout from your decisions.

Now you have finished the four sentences above you should have a good idea of what formed your trust in one another. Now think about how you appreciate trust in one another every day. Here is a list of things that successful couples do to maintain trust in their relationships.

✓ Keep promises – large and small.

✓ Listen to what their partner feels.

✓ Express their own feelings in a loving way.

✓ Respond appropriately to any given situation. For instance, they do not exaggerate a difficult situation into a catastrophe or minimise as unimportant something of importance to their partner.

✓ Explain why he or she intends to take the action they want to.

✓ Do not keep secrets.

✓ Take account of the roots of trust in the partnership. For instance, they remember what hurt or pleased their partner in the past and try to avoid or repeat these behaviours in the future.

✓ Take action that reflects the shared notion of trust in the rela-tionship, even when alone. For instance, they behave with integrity when away from their partner.

✓ Never manipulate a partner into doing something they feel is wrong.

✓ Are honest, but sensitive, when asked for an opinion.

Reading this list you may be surprised to see some of the items. For instance, 'expressing your feelings in a loving way' may seem unconnected to trust. But if you can do this, your partner will develop a sense of trust in your ability to share your thoughts and emotions without fear of being battered by your opinions or having to drag information out of you. Similarly, 'explain why he or she intends to take the action they want to' allows you to follow their thinking process. This helps you to develop trust in your partner because you will understand their motivation for whatever they wish to do. Read the rest of the list and decide if you can apply each point to your relationship. If you cannot, ask yourself what it would take to put it in place. If you struggle with lots of the items on the list, your relationship may need an overhaul because you are missing the basic commodity of a trusting relationship – a sense of belief in your partner.

How not to be boring

Predictability has become a dirty word in lots of couple relationships. Nowadays, to be predictable suggests you are really boring, living a life caged by routine rather than exploring interest and excitement. Yet predictability is crucial to all human relationships. If your partner behaved extremely erratically, coming home only when he or she felt like it, behaving lovingly one minute and horribly the next, you would soon wonder if you had a relationship worth keeping. Everyone needs predictability to run his or her life. Watch the average TV soap and you can see what unpredictability does to a family! This might add to the dramatic tension on screen, but in real life would feel like a dangerous roller coaster ride to misery. So being predictable does not have to be boring. It means allowing your partner to know that you are likely to behave in a way that he or she feels safe with.

If your partner finds it hard to be predictable, they may fear making a commitment to you. In fact, they are deliberately sabotaging your attempts to know them. This sets up a smokescreen of uncertainty that stops you feeling secure, preventing the partnership from ever reaching a mature level. Some people find this kind of partner a challenge, hanging on to the situation long after it is clear to everyone else that they are being taken for a ride. This is sometimes known as the 'if I love them enough they will stop behaving in this way and care for me' syndrome. Occasionally loving someone can be redemptive. They realise the error of their ways and commit for real. But more often than not they never change and you are left with an armful of empty promises and no real relationship. The truth is that predictability allows you to be free rather than eaten up with worry. So here is how to recognise predictability.

Look for somone who:

Is relatively even tempered. This does not mean they have to be emotionally stuck on one note. They will be able to show strong feeling when they need to, but do not veer wildly from one side to the other of the emotional spectrum.

Is capable of following some routine. People who cannot fit in with plans or say they feel constricted by any kind of routine may be struggling against being in a relationship. In contrast, someone who turns up when they say they will and can follow a schedule when needed generates a feeling of trust and dependability.

Matches deeds with words. The old saying 'words are cheap' is certainly true in the trustworthiness stakes. It is easy to say you will do something. Following through with action is the key result you need to look for in your partner.

Remembers what they promise. Some people can make lots of promises but never keep them. They may even promise to stop (or start) something several times. For example, suppose you want your partner to accompany you to visit a relative but each time they are mysteriously engaged elsewhere, even after a promise to go with you. You might tolerate this once or twice, but more than this can indicate they are finding it difficult to say why they will not come.

Is honest and straightforward. This links to the point above. If your partner can explain his or her thinking to you, it is much easier to know where you stand and enables trust to be shared between you.

These are all attributes you should practise yourself. It is no good expecting your partner to be predictable when you are not. Developing trust is a two-way street.

Keeping promises

If you make promises to one another, you may sometimes be mystified as to why they get broken. You may start out with lots of good intentions, only to find that things go awry somewhere in the process. If you recognise this pattern, here is how to make promises stick:

- *Never assume you know what is expected.* Saying 'Yes, I promise I will do it' when you have only half listened to the request because you were watching TV does not constitute a promise. Make sure you know what you have agreed to.

- *Set the boundaries.* If there are time constraints, complications (such as having to do something in set stages) or important emotional reasons (such as the importance of buying a birthday card for your mother), make sure you know them or explain them. A vague suggestion will almost ensure the promise gets forgotten or ignored.

- *Explain why you need ask for the promise.* Some promises get broken when the person who is asked to carry them out cannot see the reason for the promise in the first place. If it is an emotional promise (rather than a physical action) you may need to be very clear about why you are asking. For example, you may want to ask your partner to always telephone you when they are late home from work because you were once very frightened when a previous partner failed to come home.

- *Agree the promise is important.* If only one of you thinks the promise is worth making, chances are nothing will happen. For instance, Nathan thought his girlfriend's suggestion that he should promise to always wash up his own plate after a late-night meal was a waste of time. He thought it should be done in the morning with the breakfast crockery. His girlfriend became more and more frustrated because Nathan did not explain why he left his plate on the drainer most nights.

- *Have a measurable outcome.* Decide what the outcome might look like. For example, if one of you promises to keep the garden tidy, talk about what this actually means. Does it mean just cutting the grass, or weeding, pruning and planting as well? This may sound a bit like overkill, but the devil is in the detail. If you do not know what you are expecting or expected to deliver, you can end up having big rows over simple things.

- *Develop a 'broken promise' strategy.* Everybody breaks a promise sometimes. Sheer forgetfulness causes most broken promises. Talk about how you will handle this kind of thing before it happens. Will you simply say 'let's try again', abandon the idea, or attempt the promise from a different angle? Lots of people use promises as tests. 'If they get this right it means they love me.' A broken promise can take on mythical proportions in your mind that your partner has completely failed to appreciate. Talk about what the promise means to you rather than puzzle over their lack of appreciation of its importance when they forget.

- *Be understanding.* Some promises will fall by the wayside despite a strong mutual desire to keep them. If this happens, forgive yourselves and try again. If you cannot keep a promise, despite your best efforts, it may simply be too high a hurdle and impossible for the two of you. It is better to accept this and move on than beat yourself up over something you have been unable to manage.

Different kinds of promises

Promises break down into two types – loaded and unloaded. Loaded promises are those that have a great deal depending on them – wedding vows, to care for children, to behave differently, and so on. When these get broken you are likely to feel hurt and let down in a serious way. This is a betrayal of your trust and you will feel sad, angry, bemused and anxious.

Unloaded promises are usually day-to-day issues – to wash up, write a letter, bath the baby, etc. They can be broken and not much will be lost except your patience and time. They can cause rows, but are usually forgotten quickly. The exception to this is when you ask for unloaded promises to be kept and they are repeatedly undone. This can seem like a lack of commitment if it happens lots of times over weeks and months. When this happens, unloaded promises can quickly become loaded ones, with each request becoming a test of honour.

Dealing with broken loaded promises

Dealing with a broken loaded promise can seem an enormous task. If you have been through the shock of the discovery of an affair, a credit card run up to the limit or evidence of drinking when you thought the problem was solved, it can seem almost impossible to recover from. But lots of couples do recover from these seemingly overwhelming problems. A recent Relate survey found that two-thirds of couples who said there had been an affair in their relationship stayed together. Some couples manage by sweeping the problem under the carpet. The trouble with this approach is that the bump in the carpet eventually trips you up! If you are going to deal with the broken promise effectively, there are better ways to deal with it than ignoring it. Use these ideas to help you resolve your problems:

- *Look for the trigger*. If one of you has broken a big promise, there will be a reason why it happened. It may seem tempting to think it was an impulse or 'out of character' aberration but every issue like this has an unacknowledged motivation. Look for bereavements, job losses and promotions, problems with kids and important birthdays (reaching the age you were when your mum or dad died or left home, for instance, can cause people to behave differently), in fact anything that may be important that you have not talked about much or thought you had put behind you. These events are pretty much the 'smoking gun' of broken loaded promises. Finding the trigger alone will not solve the difficulty but it will help you both to face the issue head on, which is what is needed if you are to recover.

- *Do not make snap decisions.* Lots of people say that when they discover a broken promise of this kind they just want to run. They may tell their partner to leave or pack their own bags. But this is a mistake. If you up and go immediately, you have no time to assess what has really happened or hear your partner's explanation. It is true, you may not like what you are going to hear but it is important to get the whole picture before you make a decision. If possible, try to remain calm and listen to what your partner has to say. One of your first responses is going to be anger. Instead of shouting and yelling, say how angry you feel and how let down you are. Engage with your partner so that they can see and hear how upset you are. The problem with banging doors and yelling insults is that your partner can use it as an excuse to shut you out emotionally. If you keep as calm as you can but say what you are feeling, they have to pay attention and cannot say 'I will only listen when you are rational'. Calmly keep telling them how you feel until they get the message.

- *Give yourself three days to take in what has happened.* Why three days? Three days is enough time for you to grasp the complexities of what has gone on, to hear what your partner has to say and for the first element of shock to die down. It is crucial that the period of shock that everyone suffers after bad news (it happens after a death as well) has time to calm down a little. Only when this has happened can you take in what you need to in order to tackle the problem. You will also have had two nights' sleep to restore your sense of balance. Your first night's sleep is likely to be poor so you will be tired by the time you get to your second night and ready to rest. By the fourth day you will feel more with it, less numbed by the news and more able to think and talk about what you want to do.

- *Find one small thing you can do together to start to restore your relationship.* Even if you think you may not stay together, there are important things you need to do if you are going to break up. You may share a home, have children, or leave personal items at each other's homes. If you are at daggers drawn for weeks, these will get poor attention and cause you much unhappiness. If you are going to stay together, you need to find something that will take you a step forward into the future. For instance, if you have discovered your partner has a huge debt on his or her store card, try chopping the card up. This will not solve the debt, but will help you both to feel it cannot happen again, at least in the short term. Essentially, something like this is a ritual that will help you both to begin rebuilding shattered trust.

- *Look at all your options.* In this situation most people jump to black and white conclusions – stay or leave being the most common one. But if you want to make a decision of most benefit to both of you, it is useful to identify everything you might want to do. For example, if one has had an affair, write lists of everything you might do. Stay together, split up permanently, go to counselling while living apart, have a temporary separation, move house for a fresh start, etc. Put down anything that you think is at all relevant. Then cross out any that are not practical or you know would not work for you. This should leave you with a list of four or five that have possibilities. Doing this exercise can help you both to see that you are not caught in a one-way trap but can take action that will help you to make sense of what happens next.

- *Keep your promises.* Most important of all, keep your promises. If you say the affair is over, it really must be. If you say you are not drinking any more, you must have really stopped. In this early phase, your partner will be watching to see if you can keep the first promise of your 'New World Order' (after the breaking of a loaded promise). If you cannot do this simple act, then he or she may think there is little hope for the future.

If you are not the one who broke a promise, you also need to act with great integrity. Modelling how to behave is under-rated in couple relationships but can help your partner to understand what you would like to happen. Try not to do this in an 'I'm better than you' style. Just allow them to see that you are willing to be part of the new way of being together.

Dealing with broken unloaded promises

This kind of promise-breaking is usually irritating but less momentous than the broken loaded promise. Usually they are connected to mixed-up expectations or misunderstandings. Often they come about because communication is not clear or straightforward. Here is how to manage these difficulties:

- *Do not expect your partner to be a mind reader*. You may wish he or she would remember to load or unload the dishwasher, put petrol in the car or cook the evening meal without you mentioning it but if you want promises to stick, you have to make it clear what you want. Do not say 'I wish you would help me around the house. You promised you would'. Do say 'Please can you unload the dishwasher when you get home'. Be clear and concise. Do not nag or moan. Nagging often gets shut out as your partner will think 'He/she is at it again' and promptly forget what you said!

- *Do not make assumptions*. You may think your demand is perfectly reasonable but never consider if your partner also thinks so. If he or she promised to do something, was it something they were really motivated to do or was it something you thought was a brilliant idea? Make sure that promises you give each other are mutually agreed rather than forced on one or the other.

- *Try to be equal*. Lots of unloaded promises get broken because the deal seems unequal to one of you. For example, you may feel put upon if you end up bathing all the children while your partner watches their favourite soap. Or you may feel this is an equal deal if you know they are going to cook the evening meal while you, in turn, watch the news.

- *Be organised.* Routines sound more applicable to factories than families but if you want a promise to be kept, avoiding chaos will help you maintain a way forward. Keep a rota on the fridge door, make note of important dates on a diary that everyone can see and check out what is going on in your partner's life at least once a week.

- *Look for the hidden message.* If unloaded promises are constantly broken in your relationship, it is time to look for the hidden message. Why is this happening? Do they hate the task they agreed to or are they angry that you do much less than them? Talk to your partner about how they are feeling. Remember to listen carefully with an open mind. Look at Chapter Eight for more ideas on managing a happy work/life balance.

Keeping promises is one of the key attributes of a successful relationship. If you can do this, in everyday activities and in the big promises of life, such as promising to love and be faithful, then your relationship will feel secure and safe. Trust is the one thing you cannot do without in a relationship. But trust is in the proof not the promise alone. To make a loving promise stick, you must act as you say you will. Do this and you have every chance of staying together forever.

INDEX